Other books by Ted Wachtel

Author

Real Justice: How We Can Revolutionize
Our Response to Wrongdoing

The Electronic Congress:
A Blueprint for Participatory Democracy

Co-author

Toughlove

Toughlove Solutions

The Restorative Practices Handbook
for Teachers, Disciplinarians and Administrators

Restorative Circles in Schools:
Building Community and Enhancing Learning

Restorative Justice Conferencing:
Real Justice® and the Conferencing Handbook

Family Power:
Engaging and Collaborating with Families

Building Campus Community:
Restorative Practices in Residential Life

Editor

Safer Saner Schools:
Restorative Practices in Education

Dreaming of a New Reality

www.dreamingofanewreality.com

Dreaming of a New Reality

◆ ◆ ◆

*How restorative practices reduce crime and violence,
improve relationships and strengthen civil society*

by
Ted Wachtel

INTERNATIONAL INSTITUTE FOR RESTORATIVE PRACTICES
Bethlehem, Pennsylvania, USA

published in collaboration with

THE PIPER'S PRESS
Pipersville, Pennsylvania, USA

INTERNATIONAL INSTITUTE FOR RESTORATIVE PRACTICES
P.O. Box 229
Bethlehem, PA 18016 USA

Published in collaboration with

THE PIPER'S PRESS
P.O. Box 400
Pipersville, PA 18947 USA

Library of Congress Control Number: 2013905163
ISBN-13: 978-1-934355-25-1
ISBN-10: 1-934355-25-9

Table of Contents

Dreaming of a New Reality

Chapter 1
Dreaming of a New Reality

I first presented "Dreaming of a New Reality," a multimedia slide show, to an audience of 500 social workers in March 1977. I had been asked to create an inspirational keynote presentation to open a professional conference at the University of Pennsylvania in Philadelphia. While it was well received, I may have been the person most impacted, because in making the presentation I met my own need for encouragement at a time when I was often consumed with self-doubt.

The eloquent quotations of notable thinkers and the lyrics from contemporary songs reassured me that quitting my job as a young public school administrator and trying to start a school for delinquent and at-risk youth was not a foolish utopian enterprise. Concluding the slide show with the Beatles' song "Let it Be,"[1] which accompanied a sequence of my photos showing the sun sinking into the Pacific at the Oregon coast, Carl Sandburg's words summed it all up: "Nothing happens unless first a dream."[2]

I was also moved by Henry David Thoreau's prescriptive message, synchronized in the presentation with a vast three-screen panorama of a Rocky Mountain valley: "If you have built castles in the air, your work need not be lost; that is where they should be. Now put the foundations under them."[3] In that same month I filed the articles of incorporation for the Community Service Foundation (CSF),[4] the first of a series of non-profit organizations and projects that various collaborators and I would establish in the coming decades — bridges on the road to a new reality.

Susan Wachtel, my wife, and I had begun teaching in public schools in 1968. Neither punitive nor permissive, we were good at engaging students who exhibited poor behavior. We both were concerned with the increasingly inappropriate attitudes of a growing number of young people, as well as the tendency for public schools to react to those students in ways that further alienated them. This loss of social capital — the relationships that bind people together and create the trust, mutual understanding and shared values that make cooperative action possible[5] — seemed to be at the heart of the problem.

In light of our experience with difficult students and while working as volunteers at a group home for delinquent youth, we became fascinated with the question: "How do you get people who are on a negative path in life to change to a positive path, and how do you prevent the negativity in the first place?" The search for answers to that and related questions became our lifelong quest.

Our journey coincided with the work of others and has coalesced into an exciting new social science called "restorative practices."[6] In the decades since we taught public school, we found that restorative practices not only reduce criminal offenses among delinquent and at-risk youth in our CSF programs, but also improve behavior and enhance learning among the special education and alternative education students who attend our Buxmont Academy[7] schools (Chapter 2: The Worst School I've Ever Been To).

In 2000 we founded the non-profit International Institute for Restorative Practices (IIRP), in Bethlehem, Pennsylvania, U.S.A. The IIRP tagline, prominently displayed on its website[8] and letterhead, is "Restoring Community in a Disconnected World." Now an independent accredited graduate school and global training and consulting organization, to date the IIRP has worked with professionals from over 55 countries, and we have more than 300 affiliates and licensees in 16 countries (Postscript).

My colleagues and I have used restorative practices to help even the most challenging public and private schools reduce violence, crime, bullying and misbehavior (Chapter 3: Safer Saner Schools).

Restorative conferences produce positive outcomes in dealing with criminal offenses for victims, offenders and their families and friends, but especially in helping victims cope with the trauma caused by crimes (Chapter 4: Real Justice).

Family group conferences (also called family group decision-making) provide the means for families to manage their own problems more effectively (Chapter 5: Family Power).

Restorative practices create positive workplaces with a remarkably high level of morale, cooperation and personal accountability (Chapter 6: Good Company).

Most recently we brought the benefits of restorative practices to residential life in higher education (Chapter 7: Building Campus Community).

Each of these chapters demonstrates how restorative practices change the world for the better in a particular sphere of society. In the three-and-a-half decades since I presented "Dreaming of a New Reality," we now have good reason to assert that restorative practices effectively answer some of our modern societies' greatest challenges.

For example, how might schools address problematic student behavior in a way that produces meaningful and sustainable improvement? In May 2012, the principal of Freedom High School in Bethlehem, Pennsylvania, dealt with four senior students who seriously vandalized the school shortly before graduation. In the past they would simply have been punished and excluded from the graduation ceremony. Instead, the school principal, Michael La Porta, whose school began implementing restorative practices nine months earlier, asked the IIRP to provide a facilitator to organize a "restorative conference."

At the conference, the facilitator followed a "restorative script," asking each of the four students a series of open-ended "restorative questions" that allowed them to speak freely and share their feelings. The facilitator then asked similar questions of the school custodians, administrators, the boys' sports coaches, the school police officer and the students' parents. Everyone had a full opportunity to be heard.

The students told their stories, listened intently and learned how their behavior affected others, sincerely expressed their remorse and participated in deciding how they should compensate for the damage they had caused. The custodial staff explained all the problems the damage created for them. The arresting police officer shared how difficult it was to face the tearful reactions of parents when he informed them that their sons' actions were considered felonies under the law. The coaches and the parents expressed their disappointment and concern for the boys' future. The facilitator later said that there were moments when there was not a dry eye in the room.

The four students agreed to make public apologies to the faculty and student body, provide 100 hours of service at the school and come back the following school year to speak publicly to other students about avoiding similar harmful behaviors during senior week. While the local public prosecutor insisted on bringing criminal charges, the principal planned to actively support the young men through the judicial process. Because the young men took appropriate responsibility for what they did wrong, the principal made an unprecedented decision to allow them to graduate with their classmates. He later described the conference as "one of the most impressive, intense and exhausting experiences in my professional career."

Bethlehem, like most school districts, had previously followed a "zero tolerance" policy through which the school board mandated harsh responses to inappropriate behavior. But behavior was getting worse, not better. However, at the beginning of the school year, the school district superintendent, Joseph Roy, asked the IIRP to introduce restorative practices at Freedom and Liberty, the two Bethlehem area high schools.

"We can't expel our way to safer schools. We need to build positive relationships to get ourselves there."[9] In 1998, Roy had been the IIRP's first ally among public school principals when he took the risk and implemented restorative practices at Palisades High School, the school my own children attended. Impressed by the positive outcomes, he subsequently introduced restorative practices at two other southeastern Pennsylvania high schools before returning to Bethlehem in 2010, where he had previously served as an assistant principal.

Speaking of that experience in a documentary film called "Beyond Zero Tolerance,"[10] Roy said, "I learned as an assistant principal at a large, more urban high school where I suspended many, many, many people — the students who changed their behavior — it wasn't because they got suspended. It was because they developed a relationship with me. … What we've tried to do with restorative practices — it puts a conceptual framework around the ideas of building positive relationships, having respect — and allows a school to be able to look at things in a different way."

Roy further explained: "Most traditional high schools are not designed to be restorative. So you have years and years, decades and decades of traditional discipline. Because that's been the dominant culture, that's what people expect. So the challenge to change it in a school is to convince people that you can deal restoratively and you're still holding people accountable."

In September 2012 the two Bethlehem high schools reported the 2011–2012 discipline data from their first year using restorative practices: Suspensions dropped 20 percent.[11] In particular, suspensions for the most serious infractions declined dramatically: Suspensions for endangerment dropped 64 percent, for insubordination 59 percent, for physical assault on a student 75 percent, for threats, harassment and bullying 81 percent. Expulsions dropped 41 percent.[12]

I'm a pragmatist. If everything is working well, then why change anything? But most people seem to share a growing concern that things in general are not going well.

We are living in an unprecedented social experiment. We have systematically changed the patterns and connections that have characterized human life as long as there has been human life. Never before in the history of the human race have so many lived so far from their extended families. Never before have so many lived outside of traditional communities in which all the adults served as the collective parents of each other's children. Never before have so many marriages ended in divorce and divided families. Never before have so many elderly grown older, away from their families, often in unfamiliar surroundings. Never before have so many children left their hometowns for other places. These changes in living patterns and increased geographic mobility have reduced our social capital and our sense of community.

Restorative practices build social capital and have positive implications for all social settings, from families to schools to workplaces. Drawing from both liberal and conservative values, restorative practices cultivate a society based on participation and mutual self-reliance, where as citizens we take greater responsibility for our own lives. Leaders and government play a role in achieving societal well-being, but equally important is support from our own social networks: family, friends, neighbors and community.[13]

While the field of physics still searches for its "unified grand theory of everything" that can explain all physical phenomena, we have come upon a unified grand theory that explains how social entities may function best. This theory rests upon a fundamental hypothesis — that "people are happier, more cooperative and productive, and more likely to make positive changes when those in positions of authority do things *with* them, rather than *to* them or *for* them." This book shares true stories and growing evidence that support this premise — from varied fields of endeavor — in a growing social movement that is improving human behavior and strengthening civil society around the world.[14]

The Worst School I've Ever Been To

Chapter 2
The Worst School I've Ever Been To

The students were returning to the baseball field after lunch when John, one of the students from our school in Sellersville, Pennsylvania, announced loudly, "We've got to have a circle because you stole a sandwich from Mr. Roeder's store." He looked directly at a student from the visiting school group who had come earlier in the day to play baseball.

"You're going to ruin it for us," John continued. "We're going to lose our privileges, and we won't be able to go to the store for lunch. And Mr. Roeder's a good guy. You shouldn't rip him off."

"What the fuck are you talking about?" the accused boy protested weakly, knowing that John was right about his theft.

The students from the visiting school looked surprised. Most of them knew that their fellow student had stolen a sandwich from the refrigerator when the group crowded into the small store at lunchtime. What surprised them was that a student, not a teacher, was making the accusation.

Both groups of students were from two alternative schools where teenage youth were sent by juvenile court as part of their probation for delinquency or by public schools for behavior issues. But only the students from John's school understood what he meant when he talked about having "a circle." They began to sit down on the grass and urged the students from the visiting school to sit and form a circle in the middle of the baseball field.

The certainty and collective will of John and his schoolmates caused everyone from both schools, including the teachers, to sit and join the group. The staff from John's school exchanged knowing glances. Since John's arrival at the school several months ago, he had shown leadership and a willingness to take risks.

Appealing to his fellow students, John said, "I think we should all talk about how we're affected by this and what should happen. Who wants to start?"

A girl sitting next to John spoke up. "When you steal from the store, it makes me worry that you're gonna steal something from me."

Then another student said, "I like Mr. Roeder. You should go back and pay him for the sandwich you took and apologize."

Still another said, "We don't want people in the neighborhood to think we're bad kids. We've worked hard to get a good reputation."

"I didn't take nothing," the thief protested.

The comments continued around the circle while the visiting group of students stayed quiet, apparently dumbfounded by the novelty of what was happening. Only the accused youth interrupted occasionally with his denials.

In the face of persistent demands and realizing that no one believed him, the thief finally abandoned his claim of innocence and said, "I'm not going back there. That guy might call the cops."

"No, he won't," said John. "He's a good guy. Other kids have been caught stealing, but he trusts us to help keep it from happening. C'mon. I'll go with you and support you."

"Yeah, I will too," said another student.

Dismayed by both the confrontation and the offers of support, the youth resisted until one of his schoolmates said angrily, "Come on, man. I just want to play baseball. I'm sick of this whole thing. Just go say you're sorry and pay for the sandwich."

The impasse was broken and the thief succumbed to peer pressure. John and two other students accompanied him when he went back to the store to apologize and pay the owner for the stolen sandwich.

Turning Point

This incident in 1983 proved to be a turning point in the history of our Community Service Foundation and Buxmont Academy programs, the first of which Susan Wachtel and I founded in 1977 to work with delinquent and at-risk youth. The circle on the baseball field affirmed the strategies that we and our colleagues had been developing over the previous several years. What we saw that day was proof that misbehaving young people could be engaged in such a way that they themselves would take responsibility for the well-being of their own school. While CSF Buxmont school staff routinely used "groups" or "circles" to deal with wrongdoing and conflict, what delighted us was seeing one of our students courageously take the initiative and use a restorative practice — without staff support — to confront a visiting student about his negative behavior.

Just like a CSF Buxmont staff member would have done, John did not attack or condemn the culprit. Instead he orchestrated a situation in which the visitor and his peers learned how the theft affected the students at our school and about their good feelings toward Mr. Roeder, the owner of the store. John also suggested a way for the shoplifter to make things right and offered to support him in doing so.

We didn't start out using restorative practices when we opened our first school in 1977. In fact, we didn't encounter the term "restorative" until 1995. Rather, when Susan Wachtel and I started, we were thinking like educators, hoping that our creativity, enthusiasm and dedication would create a school setting that would entice students to learn and behave appropriately. But we quickly came to the realization that running an exciting school program was not enough. Our students were restless, impulsive and often drug-abusing. They had disdain for authority and punishment. They had not changed their behavior in their home schools when sanctioned with detention, suspension or expulsion. They had reached the point where they didn't seem to care about school anymore. So we had to do something different.

What we learned, over time, was to change the nature of the relationship between the adults and young people in our school. We created a community where students felt connected, respected and empowered. We insisted that they had to take on a greater share of responsibility for their own behavior, for that of their peers and for the well-being of their school, and in return they obtained a real voice in how matters were handled. Rather than simply imposing punishments, we developed strategies that made students responsible for problems that arose and for finding their own solutions. Developing these practices improved the environment in our school and produced positive behavioral changes in individual students, sometimes quickly and dramatically.

"I can't believe it," remarked a visiting public school administrator whose school had students enrolled in our program. "Is that the same kid who leaped across my desk and threatened me? That was only two months ago, and now he's leading a group of students in an activity. I can't believe it. He actually said hello to me."

What people find most remarkable is how simple our strategies are: definitely not rocket science. Fundamental to our approach is to afford students opportunities to be heard and to express their emotions appropriately. Allowing young people to express themselves reduces their emotional intensity and improves the likelihood of a civil exchange.

Usually adults do all the talking, especially when children have done something wrong. We lecture. We scold. We punish. But we rarely ask for the child's input, except when the person in authority is gathering information to figure out "who dunnit."

Presumably the visiting public school administrator had not asked for the young person's input before the student exploded and threatened him. In fairness to the administrator, he was only doing what most adults do when we are disciplining a young person — because that's how we ourselves were raised. And, of course, we should not justify or excuse the student's behavior just because he wasn't given a chance to air his views. We must still hold him accountable for how he chose to deal with his anger or frustration. But as a practical matter, in a world where outrageous behavior has become increasingly commonplace, we could all benefit by learning how to avoid and defuse conflicts effectively.

Fair Process

A key element of the IIRP's introductory courses and professional development in restorative practices is when we ask those in attendance to think of a person from their past that they respected — a teacher or a boss or any other authority figure. When we ask them to be specific about what it was that they respected about that person, particularly when that person challenged them for doing something wrong or for failing to live up to expectations, the group always reaches the same conclusion. The person they respected was firm but fair. They usually describe fairness as having the chance to be heard, express feelings and tell their side of the story.

This view is supported by research findings in business management and can be generalized to any type of social organization — from a family or classroom to a school or company. In what is now considered a classic article from the *Harvard Business Review*, the authors delineate "engagement" as the first of three principles to achieve what is termed "fair process": "Engagement means involving individuals in the decisions that affect them by asking for their input and allowing them to refute the merits of one another's ideas and assumptions." "Explanation" and "expectation clarity" are the second and third principles of fair process.[15]

Applying these three principles to a school setting means that when a student has done something wrong, she feels respected when the teacher or administrator allows her to speak. When school authorities explain their decision about what has to happen as a result of the wrong, taking into account the student's perspective, the young person feels confident that she was actually heard. And thirdly, when the teacher or administrator clarifies their future expectations, they reinforce the overall feeling of fairness.

Those in authority in any social organization who follow these three principles in exercising their leadership, whether teachers, school administrators, business managers or parents, will find that their students or employees or children will be more likely to cooperate when they feel that they were treated fairly, whether or not they get the decision they wanted.[16]

As we developed our strategies at the first CSF Buxmont school in the late 1970s and early 1980s, we were also unknowingly mirroring findings from research conducted only a few years earlier in the psychology of justice. This research established that people care as much about the fairness of a judicial process as they do about the outcome of a process. The extent to which they have a voice in the proceedings has a strong effect on their perceived sense of fairness and on their likelihood to follow rules voluntarily.[17]

Restorative Questions

Engagement, however, need not be only about having a voice to express one's own feelings and perspective. In our schools we also engage students in processes that expose them to the feelings of those they have affected, something that doesn't happen when the authority simply hands out punishments. For example, one of the ways that we can engage wrongdoers is to ask a series of restorative questions.[18]

Restorative questions stand in stark contrast to the useless question so often asked by adults when a young person has just done something wrong: "Why did you do it?" Rarely do offending children know "why." Usually their actions were thoughtless and impulsive, without any rationale whatsoever. So they typically shrug and answer, with their eyes directed toward the floor, "I dunno."

Instead, restorative questions are designed to engage young people in a reflective process, where they, not the adults, have to do the talking and solve the problems. These questions are similar to the questions asked in a restorative conference.

The first set of questions are asked of the person whose behavior has caused the problem:

> ➤ What happened?
> ➤ What were you thinking about at the time?

> What have you thought about since?
> Who has been affected by what you have done? In what way?
> What do you think you need to do to make things right?

The questions should be followed by patient pauses to allow time to answer. The silence provides a gentle form of pressure. Where children or youth are particularly shy or inarticulate, some prompting or clarifying of questions can help them along their way.

Another set of restorative questions should be asked of those who were affected by the young person's actions, to acknowledge the harm done to them, to expose the offending young person to the impact of what they have done, and to give the person who has been affected a say in how things will be resolved:

> What did you think when you realized what had happened?
> What impact has this incident had on you and others?
> What has been the hardest thing for you?
> What do you think needs to happen to make things right?

These are not the only possible questions to ask following an incident, just suggested questions that have proved helpful and effective in a wide variety of situations. We have found them to be so effective that we publish and popularize them as the "restorative questions," printing them on wallet-size cards, posters and A-frame signs.[19]

Of course, one has to use good judgment about when to ask the questions. In the heat of the moment, when emotions are running high, is not the opportune time. Rather, waiting until everyone has settled down is more appropriate.

Restorative Milieu

Asking restorative questions is only one way to be restorative. Restorative practices can take a great many forms, from spontaneous informal interventions to structured formal processes. The more formal practices are called "restorative circles" or "restorative conferences," and they take more time to arrange and conduct. Some restorative practices involve the use of restorative questions while others do not. Some are reactive, as a response to wrongdoing. Others are proactive, engaging participants in activities that build a sense of community through the development of relationships. In our CSF Buxmont schools, group homes and other programs for delinquent and at-risk youth, the repetitive use of a wide variety of restorative interactions creates what researcher Paul McCold called a "restorative milieu."[20] The milieu represents the consistent manifestation of the restorative credo of doing things *with* people, rather than *to* them or *for* them.

The most informal restorative interaction is a simple affective statement in which one person lets another know how he or she is feeling about something that person did. An example of a proactive interaction that affirms a relationship might be when one of our CSF Buxmont teachers says to a student, "I am very pleased with the way you handled your anger. You were upset, but you didn't fly off the handle. You stopped yourself and said what concerned you calmly. Great job."

On the other hand, when reacting to inappropriate behavior, one of our staff might say, "Jason, you really hurt my feelings when you act like that. And it surprises me, because I don't think you want to hurt anyone on purpose." In some instances, that may be all that needs to be done to get the student to change his behavior. Young people are often surprised that adults have feelings, especially adults they see as authority figures. If a similar behavior happens again, we might simply repeat the response or try a different restorative intervention. We might ask a question such as, "How do you think others in the class felt when you did that?" and then wait patiently for an answer.[21]

A more elaborate response to wrongdoing is the small impromptu conference. Some years ago I was with the CSF Buxmont residential program director, awaiting a court hearing about placing a 14-year-old boy in one of our group homes. His grandmother told us how on Christmas Eve, several days before, he had gone over to a cousin's house without permission and without letting her know. He did not come back until the next morning, just barely in time for them to catch a bus to her sister's house for Christmas dinner. The program director encouraged the grandmother to talk about how that incident had affected her and how worried she was about her grandson. The boy was surprised by how deeply his behavior had affected his grandmother. As a result of this impromptu conference he readily and sincerely apologized.[22]

Circles or group processes are used proactively or reactively, to build community or to respond to wrongdoing, but they are still less structured and require less preparation than a formal restorative conference. Some years ago two boys got into a fistfight, an unusual event at the CSF Buxmont schools. After the fight was stopped, their parents were called to come and pick them up. If the boys wanted to return to our school, each boy had to phone and ask for an opportunity to participate in a circle, convincing the staff and his fellow students that he should be allowed back. Both boys called and came to school. One refused to take responsibility and had a defiant attitude. He was not re-admitted. The other was humble, even tearful. In the circle he listened attentively while staff and students told him how he had affected them, willingly took responsibility for his behavior and got a lot of compliments about how he handled the meeting. He was re-admitted and no further action was taken. The other boy was sent to the juvenile detention center by his probation officer.[23]

The cumulative result of all of this affective exchange in a school is far more productive than lecturing, scolding, threatening or handing out detentions, suspensions and expulsions. Our teachers, many of whom are former public school teachers, often tell us that classroom decorum in the CSF Buxmont schools for troubled youth is routinely better than in the public schools where they had previously worked.[24]

Affect and Shame

The most critical function of restorative practices is restoring and building relationships. Because informal and formal restorative processes foster the expression of affect or emotion, they also foster emotional bonds. The late Silvan S. Tomkins's writings about the "psychology of affect" assert that human relationships are best and healthiest when there is free expression of affect or emotion — minimizing the negative, maximizing the positive, but allowing for free expression.[25] Donald Nathanson, former director of the Silvan S. Tomkins Institute, added that it is through the mutual exchange of expressed affect that we build community, creating the emotional bonds that tie us all together.[26] That has been key to engaging sometimes defiant and hostile young people as they enter CSF Buxmont. Through circles and other restorative practices they are quickly drawn into a feeling of belonging and community.

Tomkins identified nine distinct affects (Figure 1) to explain the expression of emotion in all humans. Most of the affects are defined by pairs of words that represent the least and the most intense expression of a particular affect. The six negative affects include *anger-rage, fear-terror, distress-anguish, disgust, dissmell* (a word Tomkins coined to describe "turning up one's nose" in a rejecting way), and *shame-humiliation. Surprise-startle* is the neutral affect, which functions like a reset button. The two positive affects are *interest-excitement* and *enjoyment-joy.*[27]

Shame is worthy of special attention. Nathanson explained that shame is a critical regulator of human social behavior. Tomkins defined shame as occurring any time that our experience of the positive affects is interrupted.[28] So an individual does not have to do something wrong to feel shame. The individual just has to experience something that interrupts interest-excitement or enjoyment-joy.[29] If you are enjoying a conversation with someone at a party and that person looks away while you are talking, perhaps when she notices a friend entering the room, you will experience a brief feeling of shame because of the interruption of your positive affects, not because you did something wrong.

Nathanson has developed the compass of shame (Figure 2) to illustrate the various ways that people react when they feel shame.

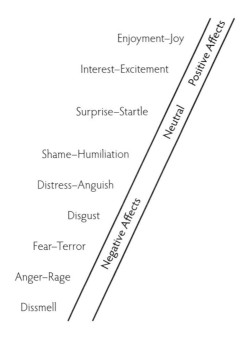

Figure 1. Nine Affects (adapted from Nathanson).[30]

There are four poles of the compass of shame and behaviors associated with them:

> *Withdrawal* — isolating oneself, running and hiding
> *Attack self* — self put-down, masochism
> *Avoidance* — denial, abusing drugs, distraction through thrill seeking
> *Attack others* — turning the tables, lashing out verbally or physically, blaming others

Nathanson says that the *attack other* response to shame is responsible for the proliferation of violence in modern life. Usually people who have adequate self-esteem readily move beyond their initial feelings of shame. Nonetheless we all react to shame, in varying degrees, in the ways described by the compass. Restorative practices, by their very nature, provide an opportunity for us to express our shame, along

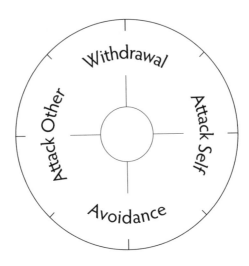

Figure 2. Compass of Shame (adapted from Nathanson).[31]

with other emotions, and in doing so reduce their intensity.[32] That is how, in our CSF Buxmont programs, we can manage behavior. In fact, we teach students about the nine affects and the compass of shame, so they can better understand and thereby cope with their own emotions.

Tim's Year at CSF

About the same time that McCold's research began at CSF Buxmont in 1999, we launched a major video project, recording the academic year in one of our CSF Buxmont schools in Lansdale, Pennsylvania. The result was an hour-long video that opens abruptly with a student named Tim exclaiming, "This is the worst school I've ever been to!" This quote, which provided both the title for the film and this chapter, is an excerpt from the first of four interviews filmed with Tim as the school year progressed.

In the "Worst School" video, Tim begins the school year as a troublemaker. When a group of students vote on defining the norms for the lunchroom in the coming year, Tim refuses to participate. He also refuses to help with routine chores. In the restorative circle that is convened on the first day of school to deal with his behavior, Tim sits with a bowed head. A student who has returned from the previous school year says to him, "The way I see you acting right now, I acted the same way. And I see how childish that is and how immature that is. It turns me off to your whole personality."

However, in a circle the next day, one of the staff praises Tim for cooperating with the chores, saying, "You got a lot of hard feedback yesterday, and you were really put on the spot, especially for the first day. And I just think it's real important to recognize that you turned things around. And you took care of things today." He receives applause from the other students for his cooperation.

In his second interview, a couple of months into the school year Tim says, "It's totally demented. The school is totally demented. It's a new kind of school for me. I'm used to work all day, none of this group bullshit, and just sticking to myself. Here I got to actually open up and talk to people."

In another circle later in the year, Tim checks in with the other students, explaining, "I was out of the program because I broke the Cardinal Rule about no threatening."

Breaking a Cardinal Rule represents a significant behavior problem, such as threatening or violence, which jeopardizes a student's participation in the program. But being "out of the program" is not like a public school suspension when a student is sent home for a couple of days. Rather, the student is removed from the school's daily activities to work out a plan to return to the mainstream. The student is not removed for a specific length of time — just until he or she can come up with a convincing plan to return. In that respect, the student has a certain degree of control over the situation. The plan usually involves a sincere apology to those who were affected by the wrongdoing and ideas about how to handle a similar situation differently the next time. In Tim's case he told the group, "I would like to apologize to the whole group for making you hear that and go through that. I would like to especially apologize to Nate. ... Next time I plan on either walking away or going up [to talk] to a staff member or to another student."

In a group circle where students spontaneously decided to share feelings and experiences about their families, Tim poignantly reveals how he deals with his often absent and abusive father. "All I got to say is I know there's people in here who are just like me. I act the way I do so — I can't let people get close to me. Because when I was younger, I let family get to me, and they hurt me. So I act the way I do, so they can't get close to me."

In his third interview, about half way through the year, Tim says, "It still sucks. This place still sucks. The worst school I've been in. What are my goals at CSF? To get my diploma and get the hell out of high school."

In another self-revealing circle Tim says, "I somewhat know my father and I somewhat don't. Because he was in the military and he's moved all over the place. Now he's down in Tennessee, so I don't talk to him. … When I was younger, the times I do remember him, he was either beating the crap out of me, my mom, my brother or my sister. The times I do talk to him, it's like — I don't want to, but he's my father. I can't help it. And I deal with it like Jeannie does. I hold it in, and finally, when I get pissed, I let it out on everybody."

In the latter half of the year Tim has a bad attitude and experiences setbacks, including a relapse into substance abuse. A girl in his group confronts him: "I think they need to put you on a stricter contract. Because you obviously don't care, and you obviously don't want to work through anything. This is the old Tim that we're seeing. The Tim that we saw in the beginning is what we're seeing now. Not the Tim that we saw in the middle, where you were working and you were on student council. And you wouldn't get smart with anybody and curse everybody out. And you actually cared. I think if you want to grow up and if you want to graduate whenever you're supposed to, I think you need to stop acting like this."

Tim pulls himself together in the last quarter of the school year and returns to his positive attitude and being a school leader. When some of his classmates are struggling with the concept of mutual responsibility for behavior and are challenging the school's demand that everyone must confront misbehaving classmates, Tim gets involved.

One of the staff says, "So as a community, you guys need to decide. When the teacher writes down that two people did not do anything in class, how does the group support those people and the teacher?"

A dissenting student challenges her: "I think that if somebody screws up, like Brian said, it should be on them. It shouldn't be on us. If you had nothing to do with it, you know?"

Tim speaks up in support of the school. "I can answer your question with one word. It's a community. No matter what the problem is, we all got to solve it for all of us to get on. As much as I hate the group [process] and as much as I think this place sucks, this place is actually getting you ready for the outside world."

In his final interview in the film Tim says, "I don't think CSF actually provided me with anything. I just think they encouraged me to do my best, no matter what it was. I am signed up to go to tech school next year, which is ATC, Automotive Training Center. Everything is paid for. I'm definitely going."

In the end-of-year awards ceremony a staff person holds up a framed award for the "most improved student." He jokes and talks about the winner and about his negative impression of the winner when the staff person first met him at his Individual Service Plan (ISP) meeting at the beginning of the school year.

"We were at the ISP with him. He said three words the entire meeting. Those were 'I don't care.' In the past month, I've seen a super change in him. He's really taken responsibility for his future and getting things together."

He announces Tim as the winner to enthusiastic applause by the class. Tim comes forward, accepts his award and hugs the staff person.

During the morning of the final day of the school year, before the afternoon's graduation ceremony when Tim will receive his high school diploma, he participates in "the Vortex." This ritual takes place in a darkened room and creates a dramatic opportunity for final remarks and good-byes. Staff and students follow each other in a serpentine line until someone decides to call out "stop" to halt the moving lines of people so that he or she is able to say something to a person standing opposite.

One of Tim's classmates stops the Vortex in front of him. He says to Tim, "Since the beginning of the year, you've always been kind of stubborn. Since the end of the year, you've been really opening up and stuff. ... Basically, I just want to wish you good luck with your job and graduating and with all the stuff you have. I just hope you succeed."

Tim acknowledges him, "Thanks." And then someone else says loudly, "You're still stubborn."

Tim laughs and snaps back, "Don't tell me that."

A few minutes later Tim stops the Vortex to speak to Karen Engle, the school's administrator: "This ain't just for you. This is for all the counselors. I just wanted to say to you all, thanks for being there. For everything I've done."

Choking with emotion he says, "You pushed me hard to do what I did. For being there when I have problems to talk about. Be it my personal life, my school life, anything. Having myself open up harder. I just want to say, 'Thank you.'" He and Karen, now both in tears, exchange hugs.

What Works and What Doesn't Work?

I am neither a bleeding-heart liberal nor a hard-nosed conservative. Rather, I'm a pragmatist. I just want to know "What works?" If punishment worked to change behavior in a lasting way, I would support the use of punishment. But there is no evidence to show that punishment reliably improves people's behavior.

Yes, punishment does influence behavior, but only when someone is watching. You can usually intimidate people and get them to conform to behavioral demands when they expect that someone will respond with unpleasant consequences. But how do you get people to internalize a commitment to behave well? How do you get people to behave well when no one can see them, when there is no likelihood of punishment?

Tim and the other young people who are sent to CSF Buxmont schools have been punished time and time again — in their homes, in schools and by the courts. Yet upon arrival Tim made it clear how he felt about us and our program. He said, "I don't care." So if we had simply relied on punishments like suspensions and expulsions, he would have continued to misbehave.

What helped Tim change his life is at the heart of restorative practices. It is what he complained about — yet what benefited him most. He and all of the students had "a voice." They had both the opportunity and the obligation to talk and to listen to others. That is what made the difference, developed the relationships and created the caring environment.

Maybe Tim didn't care when he arrived, but he started to realize how he was negatively affecting others, especially his peers, and that they were not going to tolerate his nonsense. He also started to realize that others wanted to hear from him — that they truly cared about what he was thinking and feeling. That's when he began to care. That's when he began to behave well — because he wanted to please others who cared about him. That's when he felt a sense of belonging to a group, an obligation to a community.

Seven years later, in 2007, Tim returned to videotape a testimonial that was posted on the website for the 30th anniversary of the CSF Buxmont programs. He talked about the impact of CSF and its staff on his life:

"They did make it easier for me to talk ... they did let me see life in a new way ... 'cause at the time I did drugs, I did alcohol, I did everything I shouldn't of. ... My priority in life right now is the health of my family. ... Now I'm taking care of people who depend on me."[33]

When he attended the CSF Buxmont School, Tim would not have known the term "restorative practices." But empirical research has confirmed that he and thousands of other young people who participated in CSF Buxmont programs have benefited from the positive impact of restorative practices.

Evidence

We asked Paul McCold, a criminal justice research scientist, to evaluate our CSF Buxmont programs. He warned us that during the preceding decade, in which he evaluated over 50 youth-serving programs for the New York State Division of Youth, he had been unable to find sufficient evidence to show that any of those programs changed the behavior of the young people they served. So we were delighted when, in the first evaluation of 919 youth discharged during the 1999–2001 school years, McCold found that the CSF Buxmont schools produced positive results in youth in three key performance measures. The "restorative milieu," as McCold termed the environment in our schools, delivered high program completion rates, positive changes in attitude and — most significantly — *cut offending in half* among young people who were in our school program for three months or more.[34]

In a second evaluation of 858 youth discharged during the 2001–2003 school years, the group repeated the original finding of a significant reduction of more than 50 percent in criminal offenses. Also, the first group of young people in the initial study, now two years later, still demonstrated a significant reduction in offending.[35] McCold concluded, "The empirical results of these two studies provide strong scientific evidence that *prolonged involvement in a restorative milieu can dramatically reduce reoffending.*"[36]

A third, much larger evaluation with 2,151 youth during the 2003–2006 school years, including young people from CSF Buxmont's residential and in-home services, again confirmed *the power of our restorative milieu to more than halve offending rates.*[37]

The positive research outcomes[38] encouraged us to believe that we were headed in the right direction in our quest for solutions. We now knew that the restorative milieu we had created in each of our schools helped young people change for the better. We were confident that these same strategies would be helpful in other school settings.

Safer Saner Schools

Chapter 3
Safer Saner Schools[39]

Even before we had research results affirming the value of restorative practices in CSF Buxmont programs, Susan Wachtel and I had observed such improvement in young people's behavior that we wanted to explore the use of restorative practices in public school settings. At first we trained educators in the use of formal restorative justice conferences, as a response to wrongdoing — but educators complained that it was difficult to use such a time-consuming process, except on rare occasions. As our knowledge and experience grew, we shifted our focus to include more informal and immediate responses to wrongdoing, as well as proactive restorative practices. That's when public schools began to show greater interest in restorative practices. We began providing training and consulting in schools near our home, in Palisades School District in Pennsylvania, where our two sons and our daughter had gone to school.

"I believe something happened to you recently, something that involved these three girls. Can you tell us about that?"

The assistant principal, Deborah Alder, is sitting in a circle with four pre-teenage girls and asks one of them to describe what happened to her.

"On Tuesday I received a picture, my school picture, and it had some drawings on it that upset me."

Each of the other girls readily takes responsibility for what they had done to her school photo.

"I drew over your face and drew a mustache."

"I drew the devil ears and the devil tail, and it was my idea to do it."

"I put the white-out on it and did the scribble."

"I feel bad because I don't really know you."

Without punishment or scolding, the assistant principal simply asks, "Now the question is, how are you going to fix it?"

As all the girls fight back tears and one responds, "If we see something happening like this again, that we try and stop it, because we know what will probably end up happening."

Another adds, "We just wanted to make sure that your feelings are OK. We didn't want to hurt them. We never intended on it."

This conversation, which takes place at Palisades Middle School, is from the opening scene of an IIRP documentary film, "Beyond Zero Tolerance: Restorative Practices in Schools," featuring circles, conferences and one-on-one meetings and interviews with students, teachers and administrators in the U.S., the Netherlands and the United Kingdom.[40]

As the assistant principal in the film asserts, "We want to raise kids who can work out their problems and work out their differences and learn to coexist, instead of shoving somebody or hitting somebody. We hear that from the workforce all the time. Kids have to be able to know how to cooperate. I can teach them anything, but they have to know how to get along."

The school principal, Edward Baumgartner, concurs: "Because there's never been a real solution to the problem of student misbehavior, we've embraced a lot of new things when they come down the pike, in hopes of finding something that really works. Well, we finally found something that really works. And that's called restorative practices."

The Failure of Zero Tolerance

The documentary presents restorative practices as an alternative to the "zero tolerance" strategies that have become commonplace in schools. A 2008 report issued by the American Psychological Association (APA) found that zero-tolerance policies in use throughout U.S. school districts have neither been effective in reducing violence nor in promoting learning. The report asserts that zero tolerance can actually increase bad behavior, lead to higher dropout rates and increase referrals to the juvenile justice system for infractions once handled within the schools. According to the report, the severe punishment of all misbehavior and infractions of school rules, no matter how minor, does more harm than good because it poisons relationships in the school community.[41] The APA called for a change in these policies and indicated a need for alternatives. Restorative practices provide an alternative, holding students accountable for their behavior, but in a respectful and supportive way that maintains students' dignity and good relationships with staff.

The National Longitudinal Study of Adolescent Health (also known as the "Add Health Study"), a large federally-funded research project involving a nationally representative sample of 83,074 students from 127 schools, found that where the school environment promotes "connectedness" there are significant positive outcomes among students, such as less violence, less drug and alcohol use and less teen pregnancy. The Add Health Study found that the need to feel that one belongs to and is cared for at school is one of the most crucial requirements for student health and well-being. On the other hand, harsh discipline policies undermine school connectedness and create animosity and fear among youth and adults.[42]

According to an analysis of the study, "Zero tolerance policies, which mandate harsh punishment (usually expulsion) for the first occurrence of an infraction, seek to make schools safer. Yet students in schools with harsh discipline policies report feeling less safe at school than do students in schools with more moderate policies."[43]

So how do we get beyond zero tolerance? My wife and I have become increasingly convinced that teacher preparation programs at colleges and universities, in terms of classroom management, are preparing teachers for a world that doesn't exist anymore. Rude and unruly students who defy authority are no longer the rare exception, even in affluent communities with a high percentage of motivated, college-bound students. In schools everywhere there are individual students who will challenge teachers and disrupt their classes.

How do you help teachers learn to engage students like Tim, who have reached the point where they "don't care"? How do you achieve good behavior without relying on intimidation and punishment, which may temporarily get compliance from most students, but not the kind of voluntary cooperation teachers would love to achieve?

Palisades School District

Consider the classic problem of student misbehavior when a substitute teacher fills in for the regular teacher. The "Beyond Zero Tolerance" documentary shows excerpts from an actual circle run with students at Palisades High School, confronting students in the class about their inappropriate behavior on the day their teacher was away.

"There was a problem the other day. Mrs. Horn was out. She had expectations for your behavior, both academically — what you were going to produce — and behaviorally — how you would treat the substitute teacher. And those expectations weren't met."

The circle provides students a chance to talk honestly about what happened and how they could help to avoid the problem in the future. One of the students admits, "I guess I shouldn't have done that. I should have tried to stop him. But I was having too much fun, so I didn't. I guess it affected the class and the student teacher. I think we all need to act like each other's babysitters."

Most adults are amazed by how cooperative students can be when presented with an opportunity to solve a problem. But then, most adults would have no way of knowing that, because for most of us the norm has always been for the adults to do all the talking, scold young people and hand out punishments.

Eileen Wickard, the circle facilitator in the film, explains the advantage of restorative practices: "The students will say it's OK for me to call them on behavior more readily than a student in the past who I would have to write up, send out. They would come back. They're still angry because I sent them away."

The conventional wisdom is that punishment holds students accountable — but punishment is passive. Students get punished and resent whoever punishes them. They believe that they are the victims. They don't think about how they have affected others nor how they might repair the harm they have caused nor how they might avoid the problem in the future. In truth, they do nothing. They merely *receive* punishment, with little or no thought or effort on their part.

In contrast, in the documentary we observe a discussion between the assistant principal, Richard Heffernan, and two students who had been involved in a fight a few days earlier.

"I want to do a follow-up today to make sure that everything is working the way that I expect it to and the way I hope each of you expect it will. How did things go today?"

One boy responds, "Our friends were just antagonizing both of us, trying to get us to fight again. But, as you can see, we both laid off each other."

The other explains, "A couple of people, like you said, were trying to get the flames up again, start stuff. And I took your advice and told them, 'It's over, so leave it alone.' And they listened to me. So far, so good."

Heffernan comments on his restorative response to the fight. "Bringing two students in who have a conflict, you could give them a detention, and you could have a short-term fix for a long-term problem. Ultimately, those students will end up in front of me again for something, probably the same situation. If we can take some time now to talk about what the real issue is, what the real problem is, and have them develop a plan for this not happening again. Number one, we're going to make a long-term solution to a long-term problem. And number two, we're ultimately going to save time from my end, because I won't be seeing these kids over and over again."

A challenging student describes how the assistant principal used restorative practices with her. "I got in trouble the other day for disrupting class. And he gave me the option of apologizing to the teacher, which I did. I think that I actually got in more trouble in my old school, knowing that I would get suspended, than I do here."

Heffernan provides further rationale: "Even though something wrong may have occurred, we try to turn it into a teachable moment. And part of that teachable moment is for them to take responsibility and for us to hold them accountable. But really for them to see the big picture and how they're affecting so many people and why these things aren't acceptable in society or in this building."

The high school principal, David Piperato, shares his perspective on restorative practices in schools: "Ultimately, the bottom line in education is student performance. And I believe that the way we approach discipline in school has a large impact on how students perform academically. People who spend time in this building will tell you the climate has never been better and that the fabric of this building, the culture, is a very positive one. And when you look at the discipline numbers, they've steadily declined."

Susan Wachtel, who for many years supervised the staff in all of our CSF Buxmont schools, appears in the film and offers her explanation of restorative practices and why they work so well: "I think what's being restored is the relationship, the good feelings between the people. When we screw up or mess up or do something wrong, it doesn't feel good. I don't like the feeling I have when I make a mistake. I feel badly. And the only way I can restore the good feelings is knowing that I apologized, I made good on it and that the person that I've wronged is OK with me again. Then we've been restored and also my self-respect has been restored."

Several middle school students concur with Susan Wachtel's emphasis on restoring good feelings and relationships. One comments, "I feel respected if we get sent to the student office, how they try to get us out of the jam and not just try to get us in trouble. And it helps a lot because it feels like you have a friend in there, and it's not like you're going into a dungeon or something."

Another remarks, "I'm actually getting along with a lot of people who I used to fight with. Because when you get in trouble with somebody, they try to make you friends again, like with the circles. I got into an incident last week, and I'm friends with that kid now."

The film shows two middle school students and a mutual friend in a circle held to deal with a fight. The friend suggests, "I think they should write a letter to you [the assistant principal] — both of them — saying what they're going to do to change."

One of the combatants says, "I make a commitment to stop arguing and fighting with him and to calm down when it comes to stuff like this." After the circle he explains, "It makes me feel pretty good that I have a good amount of say in what we're going to do to try and solve the problem."

Alder, the middle school assistant principal, emphasizes that "you have to trust the kids" and believe that they will do the right thing "if you give them the tools to do it and you give them the room to do it."

Baumgartner, the middle school principal, points out that discipline referrals have dropped significantly and that "there's not been one fistfight in the building this year." He adds that "the true test is if you can grow a culture where kids will self-report or report a friend, out of concern for their well-being. And that's happening."

One student summarizes the whole approach by saying, "I think we have more responsibilities, and we get to be a part of disciplining ourselves more."

Despite the positive results we achieved in the Palisades schools, we were often challenged by those who questioned whether restorative practices would work in urban schools or in schools in other countries. We soon had opportunities to put those questions to the test.

City Springs Elementary School

Rhonda Richetta, the principal at City Springs Elementary School in inner-city Baltimore, Maryland, was eager to bring restorative practices to her school. She has since become an enthusiastic advocate, traveling to numerous IIRP events to tell other school administrators about her experiences.

In the documentary Richetta says, "I want the children to understand why it is they shouldn't do the things that we don't want them to do. But to not do it because *they* don't want to do it. Because *they* feel in their heart that it's wrong. Once the children begin to learn it and understand it, they will teach each other. And the behaviors that were difficult began to disappear … and actually discipline took less time."

The documentary shows a misbehaving student at City Springs in a restorative process, being asked how his mother has been affected by his behavior — something a simple punishment would never achieve.The boy answers thoughtfully, "My mother, she works two jobs, and she doesn't have any time to come up here and check on me during the mornings or during the afternoons. And it affected my teachers, because it's hard for them to teach and give directions." He reaches the conclusion that "I need to change my behavior, and stop talking."

A critical development in our restorative practices implementation in schools was our growing emphasis on prevention. Richetta explains, "One of the biggest changes that I saw was with the teachers who incorporated this into their classroom. And that it wasn't a tool that was just used when things went wrong, but it was a tool to use to have discussions. …We just try to build a family and a community within the school. To really motivate and encourage the children."

A teacher adds, "We get in our circle. I've had them set goals for themselves, something that they wanted to do better. To help the group support each other, they gave suggestions to each other. They try to encourage each other in class now that they know what each other's goals are."

West Philadelphia High School

"The Transformation of West Philadelphia High School"[44] is a nine-minute video comprised solely of comments by administrators, teachers and students — no narration. It puts to rest the question whether restorative practices will work in the most troublesome and violent schools. The assistant principal, Russell Gallagher, begins the video by explaining that his school was considered one of the worst schools in the city of Philadelphia. It was on Pennsylvania's list of "persistently dangerous schools" until adopting restorative practices. "As a result, at the end of last year, our violent acts and serious incidents were down 52 percent, the largest change in the city. This year so far, we're down an additional 45 percent."

One of the teachers, James Cotton, describes a restorative intervention that prevented a fight: "We had two different cliques, and basically it boiled down to one girl looking at the other girl wrong. ... We sat them down and we allowed each of them to tell exactly how they were feeling about what was going on in the school. And when it was over with we found out that it was really a misunderstanding. And so everybody felt good, and we went on about our business in a positive way."

Another teacher, Marsha Walker, describes her personal quest for a better way to manage her classroom: "We punish kids but we never really talk to them. I personally have an issue with that as a teacher. Sometimes you need to talk, and that's what I think restorative practices gives us. ... I needed to find something that would help me have a different kind of interaction with my students. And the main thing that I liked initially about restorative practices was that whole idea of building a community. So in September, when we started school, the principal encouraged us to use the circles. You know, kind of just to build the family. So I started doing that in my classes and I liked it and I found that my students liked it as well. And I can feel that we have more of a family interaction this year. I can see the difference in my students, and I also see the difference in my behavior. Because I can be very aggressive, and I am very aggressive with my students, but I needed not to be."

Another teacher explains, "As a school that has a lot of social climate issues, utilizing restorative practices and building positive social culture is essential to the functioning of any school. I mean it's essential. Content and material mean nothing without relationships." He notes, "95 percent of the problems that we have are miscommunication. And so the act of communicating without using violence is a powerful act."

The principal, Saliyah Cruz, and assistant principal Gallagher describe their use of circles to help a teacher who was struggling to maintain order in her classroom: "We tried a restorative practices conference. We asked the teacher, 'Could we put the kids in a circle, and could we have them share their perception about what's happening in your class? And would you be open to hearing that?' So the teacher was very good about being comfortable with being vulnerable in that way.

"The kids took it very seriously. They had some very clear and concrete things to say about their role in the class and why they maybe weren't doing the things they should have been doing, what they saw as the teacher's role and why things weren't going the way they should go in the class. And to the teachers credit, she took notes, and she really did try to make corrections in terms of what the kids had talked about.

"I think the turning moment, and I could see it in the students' faces, was when they realized they had a say. They realized they were participants, that they were going to be listened to, they could have input."

Students in the video refer to their experience with restorative practices as "circles." Their perceptions of what changed in their school are heartfelt and compelling:

"Before we had circles at our school there was a lot of fights, riots, problems. It was just a lot of confusion."

"I think circles help because it expresses a student's feelings and stuff more. Instead of violence and stuff, just talking in a circle could avoid violence."

"Now that we have circles at our school, it is more like calm and collected, and we get to talk around our peers and staff respectfully and tell them how we feel and what's the problem."

"Circles have changed our class because we've had to talk to one another. It's not just the teachers. It's all of us together. So we've kind of had to come together as a team and talk."

"When something's bothering me circles help me relax, because I'm talking to somebody. With me, when I am frustrated or sad and all these other emotions, I need to talk to somebody."

One of the teachers concludes, "Restorative practices can work in tough urban schools, and it doesn't get any tougher than West Philadelphia High School."

Schools in the Netherlands

Shortly after 9/11/2001, the IIRP worked in two inner-city Dutch schools in the Hague. One of the principals who appeared in the documentary, Roel van Pagée, explained their schools' challenges: "We have a lot of nationalities. We have 95 percent of children who have parents who were not born in the Netherlands. I am 25 years in education now, working in all kinds of schools. And I was always searching for ways to deal with groups, because group influence is a very tough issue for children — how to deal with group pressure and so on. Restorative practices gave me the opportunity and the tools to deal with that in a very good way with very good results."

The other Dutch principal, Joke Reijman, added, "When you start talking to the pupils, they are surprised. They are used to being scolded at by adults. Adults tell them what to do. And now they have to think for themselves and find out for themselves what the effects are and how they can affect their own behavior."

Since the documentary was produced the IIRP and its affiliates have worked in schools around the world. Restorative practices are transcultural and are useful in bridging divisions between students of different cultures and in dealing with related issues, such as bullying.

Kosciusko Middle School

At Hamtramck School District, an economically disadvantaged school district in Michigan, about one-fifth of its students speak Bengali as their primary language, one-fifth speak Arabic and others speak Bosnian, Polish and Albanian — 27 languages in all. Despite the challenges of dealing with so many cultures, Kosciusko Middle School, in Hamtramck, has experienced a 75 percent decrease in bullying since the 2008–2009 school year when restorative practices were introduced. Restorative practices have also reduced discipline referrals to the office by almost two-thirds.[45]

The restorative practices coordinator at Kosciusko, Christina Adamczyk, facilitated a restorative conference in 2010 to deal with two middle school girls who had written what they called a "hit list" naming 25 fellow students they hated. Parents with children on the list said they'd been terrified, thinking that someone wanted to kill their child. In a tearful conference, conducted in Bengali, Bosnian, Arabic and English, with translators assisting communication among staff, students and parents, the two girls apologized profusely, acknowledging that they had not realized the impact of their actions. Everyone agreed that the girls should not be expelled, but they were not permitted to attend the eighth-grade class trip and had to work in the school office during the summer as a way of making amends. According to Adamczyk, "It was very powerful. Everyone shared food afterwards, speaking different languages. Parents with kids on the list went out of their way to speak to the parents of the kids who wrote the list."[46]

A 15-year-old Bosnian girl said, "Last year there was a split between African-Americans and Arabs. Now we can see there are lots of ways to communicate with each other. Now people sit together and walk down the hall together."

A 15-year-old Bengali boy talked about his middle school: "In circles you get to know each other. You can say anything that comes into your head. I felt shame at other schools. I feel good here. I never saw a school before where there was no bullying."

Collingwood Primary School

In Hull, England, one of the most economically disadvantaged cities in the United Kingdom, Collingwood Primary School's headteacher, Estelle Macdonald, explains how she has transformed her school by using restorative practices:

"When I first took over the school, nearly three years ago, the school was in special measures. Which means that the government had deemed it needing very special attention, at risk really of being closed down because things were so bad. Restorative practices helped us to make it the best it can possibly be.

"We brought the school successfully out of special measures using many of the strategies that I've come across with restorative practices. The key and fundamental part of restorative practices is building this sense of community within a school. Children are living in an increasingly disjointed world where their norms, their values and their sense of community have been eroded. And we have to find a way to build and restore that sense of community within a school. Because that's what schools are about.

"Two years after you come out of special measures, they come back to inspect you again. When they came into the school, they were really impressed with what they'd seen, and they judged us to be outstanding. Which puts us now in the top ten percent of schools in the country."

Whole-School Change Program

Even though our earliest efforts in schools produced positive outcomes, the greatest challenge is to achieve effective implementation. The most recent advance in our work in schools is a highly structured two-year "whole-school change program." Four key professional development days are followed by professional learning groups — recurring meetings of small groups of staff who review and refine their own progress toward a set of targeted objectives — the essential elements of a restorative school. We also train several veteran staff to provide professional development days for newly employed staff in the future and license the trainers with the right to use all of our educational materials, including our copyrighted videos and digital presentations.

We are dedicated to achieving comprehensive, sustainable and affordable change. We will soon employ our whole-school implementation strategy in a rigorous randomized control trial of restorative practices in schools. Nonetheless, the favorable results achieved to date in a growing number of schools have made a credible case for the value of restorative practices.

Evidence

After a decade of working in public schools, the IIRP published a report entitled "Improving School Climate," which highlighted the positive outcomes resulting from the use of restorative practices in individual schools and in whole school districts in Canada, the United Kingdom and the United States.[47] The data generally reflects both a decrease in incidents of wrongdoing and a shift away from the use of sanctions toward restorative modes of accountability. A few examples:

Pottstown High School, a small suburban school of 874 students in Pennsylvania, reduced by half the number of fights, cafeteria violations and out-of-school suspensions.

West Philadelphia High School, with 913 students, had been on the "persistently dangerous school" list for six consecutive years. The dramatic decreases in serious incidents, cited in the video by the principal, led to the high school being removed from the list.

At Kawartha Pine Ridge School District, east of Toronto, Canada, with more than 35,000 students in 82 elementary and 18 secondary schools, reported an 18 percent reduction in elementary student suspensions and a 7 percent reduction in secondary student suspensions.

Across more rural Keewatin-Patricia District School Board in Canada, with 5,500 students, the number of suspensions fell by 65 percent overall.

Besides the summary data about Hull, England, that appears in ou report, Collingwood Primary School and Endeavour High School have since provided us with more detailed data that highlights the result of using restorative practices in these two schools.

Collingwood Primary School reported:

> 98.3% reduction in classroom exclusions during lessons
> 92.0% reduction in exclusions from break
> 77.8% reduction in number of red cards at lunchtime

> 75.0% reduction in racist incidents
> 86.7% improvement in punctuality

Endeavour High School reported:
> 45.6% reduction in incidents of verbal abuse
> 59.4% reduction in incidents of physical abuse
> 43.2% reduction in incidents of disruptive behavior
> 78.6% reduction in racist incidents
> 100.0% reduction in incidents of drug use
> 50.0% reduction in incidents of theft
> 44.5% reduction in fixed term exclusions
> 62.5% reduction in total days of staff absence

In relation to the last percentage reporting the reduction in staff absences, Chris Straker, Endeavour High School's headteacher at the time, further noted that the reduction resulted in savings of £60,000 in the cost of supply teachers in the eight months following the introduction of restorative practices. (In U.S. terms: $90,000 savings in the cost of substitute teachers.)

"Somebody could have died that day"

Nonetheless, the most exciting potential of restorative practices is that young people themselves, not just their teachers, will embrace those practices in their daily lives. The following story was posted on the IIRP blog:

"Somebody could have died that day." That's what a student said after a fight nearly erupted at a small Detroit high school last month. But a restorative circle squashed the tension and prevented a tragedy.

It began in the cafeteria with an argument between two boys, but it quickly escalated, with kids taking sides, stripping off their shirts and getting into it. With some of the students claiming past affiliation with a neighborhood gang, this was serious.

The adults tried to separate the boys, but they struggled to calm the two students down.

Then a ninth grade boy stepped in: "I got this. I'll do a circle."

The adults were skeptical. But the kids were down with it. They knew what he meant. They would sit in a circle and talk about what was happening. They would handle this themselves.

These kids had been "doing circles" in their classrooms for a couple of months — from "check-ins," to circles involving academic subjects, to those dealing with problems. They knew what to do.

They pulled some chairs into a circle. The ninth-grader led the process, and the two boys and everyone else involved in the incident had their say, going around the circle, one at a time. The adults sat on the sidelines and watched and listened.

The two boys who were directly involved in the incident soon realized that their argument had been based on a silly misunderstanding, and their anger and hostility faded as quickly as it had flared up. By the end, the two boys were hugging and in tears: "You know you're my brother. I'll always have your back." Everyone else was crying and hugging, too.

Now a couple of kids pulled out their cell phones and started texting. Outside the window, a couple of cars that had been idling next to the building, whose drivers had been called to step in if a fight erupted, drove away.

An administrator said, "Adults with advanced degrees couldn't handle this. But the kids could. With restorative practices, we're empowering kids to take charge of their own lives."

Somebody might have died that day. But thanks to students learning to manage conflict with their peers, it didn't happen.[48]

Real Justice

Chapter 4
Real Justice

Reducing the Impact of Crime

"I think this has really been worthwhile, and I actually do thank you for coming because it's really given me an opportunity to begin to humanize Michael's death rather than just some statistic," says Brendon Dorff, one of the friends and family members who participated in a restorative justice conference with prison inmates Karl Kramer and Douglas Edwards. They are two of the four men who took part in an armed robbery four years earlier that resulted in the murder of 19-year-old Michael Marslew, Brendon's friend, who was working in a Pizza Hut restaurant in a suburb of Sydney, Australia. The restorative conference was the focus of a film, *Facing the Demons*,[49] which aired on nationwide public television in several countries and was named the best Australian documentary of 1999.

"I just hope this process has humanized Michael and shown that he's not just a person, but top bloke, top mate, top son and a real friend to everyone." Brendon continued, "Thanks for coming, but the resentment's obviously still there and will never ever go away. But at least this was — I've got to say, this was good for me."

Although the goal of criminal justice systems is usually defined as reducing crime, restorative justice adds a whole new purpose — *reducing the harm caused by crime*. Convicting and sentencing offenders to prison is vastly overrated in its capacity to provide healing for victims and their families because, as this chapter will illustrate, the criminal justice system does not deal with the emotional impact and trauma of crime.[50]

Nils Christie, the eminent Norwegian criminologist, wrote that our conflicts are our property. They belong to us, but the professionals associated with the courts and the criminal justice system "steal" our conflicts and, in doing so, deprive us of the benefits of being involved in the resolution of those conflicts.[51] Restorative justice, on the other hand, involves those who have been affected by a crime in processes that allow them to deal with the feelings, questions and misconceptions produced by the offense and, to the extent that it is possible, repair harm and restore relationships.[52]

Facing the Demons

Terry O'Connell, the director of the IIRP affiliate in Australia, pioneered restorative conferencing in the early 1990s while serving as a New South Wales police officer.[53] Although his earliest conferences dealt largely with non-violent crimes that were part of an effort to divert young offenders from further involvement with the criminal justice system, he also began to use the conference process with serious adult offenses. He organized and facilitated the restorative conference in *Facing the Demons* that took place more than four years after the murder, trial and incarceration of the four offenders (only two of whom chose to participate in the conference). About a year after the conference, O'Connell videotaped interviews with some of the participants to learn how they had been impacted by the experience.[54] Excerpts from both the documentary and the subsequent interviews will help the reader understand the benefits of restorative justice.

Karl Kramer, who organized the robbery, explains about how the conference came about:

"I saw a TV special that was being broadcast from a jail that had been closed down ... discussing the attitude of sentencing, victims, the judicial system in general. It was an open-forum debate. The father of the man whose death I caused — he was part of the forum. ... Near the end of the program, the presenter of the program asked one question to Ken Marslew [Michael Marslew's father]: 'Would you like the opportunity to confront the killers of your son?' And instantly, without any other thought or anything, he answered in a very assertive and very meaningful, 'Yes.' And that was it. That was the end of the program. Well, at that moment I had knowledge that this man, that's what he truly wanted, was that opportunity. I can remember walking out of my cell and thinking, 'Well, I got to find a way to give him what he wants.'"

Kramer reached out with the help of two nuns who worked in the prison and made contact with others who became involved in making the conference possible. Dee Cameron, whose company produced the documentary, collaborated with Terry O'Connell, who wanted the public to learn about the benefits of restorative conferences. As O'Connell explains in *Facing the Demons,* "The conference is simply a forum whereby those directly affected by a tragic incident, a murder — offenders, victims and their respective families — [are] able to share in a process that would allow them to feel better as a result of that experience." He persuaded Corrective Services New South Wales to cooperate with the restorative conference and the documentary.

The documentary shows O'Connell organizing the event, visiting with the potential conference participants and then opening the conference itself:

"Good afternoon and welcome. I will facilitate this restorative justice conference, which is being convened in an attempt to explore and deal with some of the impact of Michael Marslew's death. You've been invited here today because Michael's death has directly impacted on each of you in some way. The term 'restorative' is about making things right. Michael, of course, cannot be brought back, but it will be important that we all look for ways of repairing some of the harm, if that's at all possible. I'd like to ask Karl to start building this understanding by having him share what he thought when he realized Michael had been shot. Karl?"

"I just flipped out, I suppose is the only term I can come up with."

"What have you thought about since you realized that on that night Michael died?"

"I believe that I've thought about it from every possible angle, in relation to my own life, my family. But mostly, I think, over the years I've become aware of the amount of pain and suffering I've caused, mainly to Michael's family."

O'Connell turns to Doug, who was the driver and so was not in the Pizza Hut during the robbery. Terry asks, "What did you think when you realized Michael had been shot?"

"I'm not sure I understood the full impact of it until I got caught. Like, I really stuffed up [made a mistake] in a really big way."

Terry asks others what they thought when they realized Michael had been shot. Lisa, a co-worker says, "I just couldn't believe it. We were all just working and doing our jobs. And I just heard this bang and turned around and couldn't believe what I saw … not only a co-worker, but a very special friend. He was just lying there and we couldn't do anything to help him."

Two other co-workers describe their trauma, which persists more than four years later.

Says Caroline, "You just ask yourself, 'Why? Why me? Why us? Why that night?'"

"Michael lost his life," says Mikel, "and I believe more than Michael lost his life. I believe everyone here lost a piece of their life." He reveals that the hardest thing for him since has been simply "moving forward in life."

Joan Griffiths, Michael's mother, who divorced from Michael's father years before the murder, shares her perspective:

"I remember the morning after, when the police took me to the morgue. I prayed all the way in that it was a mistake, that it wasn't my baby. And his little ears were full of blood and his head. And the bullets had come through to his face. His little eyes were still a bit open, just like they were when he slept. And I thought he was asleep, so I went over to stroke him. I touched his hair, and my hands were covered with blood. He was dead. … And that's what I see every night when I go to bed. … That's what you've left me, that's my life."

O'Connell turns next to the murder victim's father, "Ken?"

"Maybe I can pose a question here." Ken Marslew queries the two offenders, "Have either of you got children?"

Karl answers, "I have."

Marslew continues, "Something that you really love and you hold closely. You kind of sit around, and you plan the future, and you see the potential that this person has. Then four maggots come out of the dark, cowardly things, and take it away just like that. How would you feel if somebody did that to you?"

The conference shifts into a succession of rapid-fire questions and comments from the friends and family of the victim, with only Karl, the more articulate of the two offenders, answering them.

"Why? Why did you do it?"

"Do you know why you did it?"

"I had no intention of taking anyone's life. There was no intent, in any way whatsoever, to take someone's life."

"Why were there six cartridges in the gun?"

"Why were there bullets in the gun?"

"Why was there a gun?"

"How can you sit there and say no one had any intent?"

"Didn't you even go over the possibilities of what might happen when you took a loaded gun?"

"Didn't you even think like, 'What if that happens?' Or did you just think, you know, 'We'll go in there and it will be OK.'"

"All four of you must carry the responsibility. None of you did anything to stop it."

"That's right, that's the whole point. I'm doing a sentence for murder because I didn't stop him, because I didn't. I'm not saying that in any way — I don't expect or want or desire any kind of understanding or diminishing my responsibility or anything like that. Especially me, because no one would have met each other except for through me. So I am, whether Vince pulled the trigger or not, I take full responsibility for taking your son's life."

"Why did you want to carry out an armed hold-up?"

"To keep property. It basically comes down to, at the time, it was to save property being lost. They needed the money for that. At that time, I was in a state of mind where I believed it was so important to me."

Joan Griffiths, Michael Marslew's mother, interjects, "How much did you expect to get from a little tiny Pizza Hut in the middle of the suburbs on a Sunday night? Between four people, what, you might have got a couple thousand dollars? Was that worth a child's life?"

"No, it wasn't. A million dollars wouldn't have been worth his life."

"Then why did you do it?"

"All you could see was dollar signs. You couldn't see anyone else in front of you, could you?"

"There's nothing I can say to you people. I don't have any excuses, none whatsoever. You will never be able to understand the justifications, the reasons and the state of mind because, like you said, we are different. I was different. You have, from what I can gather, you have a high moral character and such. So because you live your lives that way, you'll never be able to understand.

"There's nothing that I can say. There's nothing that I can do. You can't understand what was going through my mind and what was happening. The only possible way you could understand is if you were me, if you walked exactly the same shoes as me through my whole life. I'm not saying that in any justification for what I did. ... I also realize that no matter how much I try and understand the suffering that you're all going through, I can never understand because it hasn't happened to me."

"What have you got to say, Doug?"

"I thought about it a lot. It all just happened like in a daze."

"That's how we live our lives now. So don't tell us how you felt."

"I'm not trying to tell, I'm not trying to justify anything. I'll at least — if I can answer any question that ... "

"Karl, what happened when you all left the scene?"

"Doug or I asked what happened, and Andrew said, 'Vince just killed someone.' The car started moving, and I went sort of ballistic ... basically, just assaulted Vince."

"Then you must have realized what he was like," remarked Joan.

"I tried to kill him for a week."

"Well, I wish you'd succeeded."

As the exchange subsides, Terry shifts the flow of the conference to Michael's closest friends, Brendon and Sarah.

"Can I ask Brendon to tell us a bit about growing up with Michael?"

"Like everyone, when I heard it, I just couldn't believe it. How can someone that outgoing, that fun, just disappear, just be taken away? You don't believe it. You see him in the coffin and it finally sinks in. A bit of you has been just absolutely ripped away, your whole life's been ripped away. This mate that you've had, you've always had there for you, he's just absolutely gone. ... You just want Michael to come back.

"You don't feel like going on. As Joan said, your life's — you're in a daze. You just don't just don't feel like doing anything. It's like doing time all the time. Every minute of the day you feel like you're in some kind of jail. You try and push on, but then things just pop up, things just remind you of Michael. And then you just crumble, and you get back up and try again."

Terry turns and says, "Sarah, you were good mates."

She responds, "I'll never have another friend like that in the world. I never will have someone like that. It took me long enough to find him. Irreplaceable."

"So how have you managed?"

"Barely. Basically, the friends we used to hang out with, when I was with Michael, I don't see them anymore because it's too painful. It just makes it too difficult. And I even stopped visiting Joan and everything because every time I went, I couldn't function for weeks after that because it's just too... And I dropped some of my subjects at school because I couldn't go, like I just couldn't. ... Now I just basically live in my home, and I don't have much of a social life because I can't go out and stuff. It's something you're just never going to get over."

Although we generally think only of the victims and the victims' family and friends as those who have been harmed by a crime, the offenders' families are also adversely affected. Joanne Edwards sat next to Douglas Edwards in the conference circle.

Terry asks, "Joanne, how has it been as Doug's mum?"

"It's terribly hard. You're not directly responsible, but you've got to share a little bit of the guilt."

Others respond, "No, you shouldn't feel that way, Joanne."

"Doug made his own choices, Joanne. It's not your fault. It's nothing that you did wrong."

"I know I didn't do anything wrong, but it happened."

Terry interjects, "You were saying at the court… "

"I heard Joan crying, and I would've liked to go over and put my arm around her. But I didn't think it was the right thing to do. I couldn't do it. I thought she might reject me."

She looks directly at Joan, saying, "I'm so sorry. I'm so sorry you lost your son."

After a couple of hours, at the close of the conference, everyone has a chance to make final comments. Joan Griffiths had planned a symbolic act of giving the offenders a "gift."

She says, looking at Karl, "You've already got a son. Every time you look at him, you think about how I feel without my son. Think what you'd feel like if someone put a gun to the back of his head and blew his brains out. That's what I go through every day.

"I lost my best friend, I lost my son, I lost his future. I've been waiting for a lot of years to see what he's going to do with his life, and you snuffed that out without a single thought for what you did. You ran away like the cowards you are, and you think you sit here and you say you're sorry and it's going to make it all go away. It'll never go away for us.

"You're still breathing, you're still going about your day-to-day life, even though you're inside jail. We're in jail constantly. You've locked us into a pattern that we can't get out of, even if we want to, no matter how hard we try. If you could give me back my son, I could forgive you anything.

"I've brought something for you because it's Christmas. When Christmas comes and you think about your family, this is what I'll spend my Christmas day with."

She reaches into her purse and takes out a plastic bag of decaying leaves she had gathered from her son's gravesite.

"That's what's left of my son. That's what you've left me. I hope you're very proud of yourselves."

And then her ex-husband, Ken Marslew speaks.

"There's a lot more left of Michael than that. His spirit, the memories. There's much more."

He apologizes for his tears saying, "I wasn't going to do this. I was going to be a tough guy in all of this."

"For you kids that have come here today, I'm so very proud of you that you were prepared to come and confront the black monsters that's been painted for so many and see that they are just people."

Turning to Karl he says, "I'm going to be your nightmare for the rest of the time you're in jail because you are going to do something to make a difference because of what you did to Michael. Now you think about it."

Ken Marslew, after his son's death, had formed an anti-violence organization called "Enough is Enough," which now comprised his full-time occupation. He suggests that Karl do something when he gets out of prison to help him in his organization's efforts, as a way of making amends for Michael's murder.

O'Connell ends the conference by thanking the participants for coming and "for placing your trust in myself and in this process."

Immediately following the conference, refreshments are served in the next room, a critical element of the conference process, which creates an opportunity for people to chat informally and transition from the intense emotionality of the conference. The documentary shows glimpses of Karl, holding the plastic bag of leaves and talking with several of the conference participants.

Although the documentary includes a few quick reactions by some of the participants, filmed shortly after the conference, the interviews

O'Connell videotaped more than a year later are more meaningful because the interval allowed participants sufficient time to recognize and be able to talk more fully about the impact of the conference.

Karl Kramer

In his interview Karl Kramer, who was still in prison, insists, "I went there not wanting to prove anything, not wanting to convince anyone of anything, not wanting to show who I am. I went there wanting absolutely nothing for myself. Just to understand.

"The things that surprised me the most about the actual process that I was involved with is the restraint by the victims. The statements they made about me, which were an expression of their anger, were nowhere near what I expected. I expected … a torrent of abuse for the entire time that I was there. To be called and to be judged as more evil than Satan. I just expected to basically be hated and despised by everybody that was there.

"I didn't feel that. I felt their pain. I felt their hatred. But I perceived their wanting to understand, to bring closure to themselves. … I perceived that their understanding was more important to them than a witch hunt … as I'd seen in victim's impact statements in overseas trials, where that's what it was used for. It was a totally different scenario.

"Something else that totally blew me away — that even now I find it hard to understand why. And that is that a couple of the participants [Brendon and Sarah] who were actually friends of Michael, they actually listened to me. … I really didn't feel any anger from them. I didn't feel any hatred or anything. What I did feel was like an emotional question mark.

"I remember thinking to myself, these people have every right … to absolutely despise me and hate me. But they've put all that aside for knowledge and understanding. Even now, to me it shows their character. It shows their strength. In a way, they inspire me now.

"Another aspect that I … didn't guess would happen is that it would run smoothly. What I mean by 'run smoothly' is that each person, although they had so much of what they wanted to say, would give each person the opportunity to speak. I actually thought it was just going to turn into a free-for-all. And all basically directed at me. That's what I thought it was going to be.

"During the conference itself and even afterwards, I felt like I physically stood up for the first time in my life. I've read a lot of books about all different kinds of spirituality and about this power they talk about, this mystical energy that can overtake a person. ... I know this is going to sound corny or whatever, but that process, to me, showed me the reality when all these wise people say to become free. ... So when I look back on the conference, I look back at it as a spiritual event. That is, that in one instant I confronted all my fears, and I didn't turn away and back away.

"For a little bit of time I felt a bit of guilt about it. I caused this man's death, and now I've got all this benefit from it. That's not right. But yet my life's better now today than it ever was before I came to jail.

"All my life I've never taken responsibility for anything. It's always been someone else's fault. I've always ducked and weaved and tried to take the easy way out of everything. So my family members did suffer under that through my whole life. When I was involved in the conference, it restored my parents' pride in me. Probably for the first time in their lives, they were proud of me for something that I'd done."

Karl also talks about Ken Marslew's statement during the conference, "basically saying that he was going to force me — or us — to bring some good out of what we'd done. ... I didn't comment on that during the conference because that's not what I was there for ... but [after the conference] what I said to him was that he can't be my worst nightmare because he has absolutely no influence over any decision or anything that I decide to do. ... I can do absolutely nothing and be granted parole. Or if I do my full term, then that's it. My punishment is over ... that anything that I decide to do or anything that I give to the community ... is because of me. I just wanted to

— out of fairness and to let him know because I sensed that we'd know each other for a long time — is basically that I was my own person and I wasn't fearing him or anything. That's not why I was there. I wasn't trying to manipulate the system to get paroled or anything like that."

Douglas Edwards

Douglas Edwards, the driver for the robbery, had finished his prison term at the time Terry O'Connell interviewed him. Edwards struggled to express himself.

O'Connell asks, "What was the conference experience like for you?"

"It was hard. I don't know. Uncomfortable. Relief at the end. Sort of a feeling of a type of finish. I faced up. I didn't feel the court was anything to do with me taking responsibility for what I'd done … "

"What do you think others got out of the conference?"

"[They got rid of] a lot of hate, bitterness. Meeting Ken after … I think he sort of got through that and wanted to help in the end. I don't know how to explain it. … After the conference, when I met him, I felt something had been sort of resolved. … It was a different feeling after it than before it."

"How important was it to have your mother at the conference?"

"Very important for me. I had a backup when I needed it. It just made me feel a bit more comfortable. She got to tell her side of the story."

"What did you get from the experience?"

"I guess an understanding of what I actually did, the effect it had on people. A chance to see the consequences of my actions. It just gave me an understanding of what I caused, or I was a part of causing."

"How would you describe your experience?"

"If I had a chance to do it again, I'd do it. Because I felt it benefited me and the other people in some way. I think it was worthwhile, for me anyway, and for Mum."

Joanne Edwards

In her interview with Terry O'Connell, Douglas Edwards's mother, Joanne, describes the day of the conference as terrifying.

"But I felt that I had to do it. I was very disappointed that there weren't any other parents there [referring to Karl's parents] because I felt as though I needed a bit of support, and I didn't have any. I was on my own."

Of particular interest are the relationships that Joanne developed with each of Michael Marslew's parents. She explains, "When the conference was over, Ken walked straight over and said to me, 'Stand up.' And he put his arms around me and gave me a big hug. Then Joan came and crouched down near me, and she said, 'Oh, we don't blame you at all.' And she gave me a hug as well, which was very gratifying because I really wasn't involved."

Further, she says, "I had contact with Joan — rang me straight after the documentary was televised. And we had a chat. And I told her that I hadn't watched it on the television. ... I just didn't want to put myself through another week of sleepless nights. Then Ken rang me, and we had about a half-hour chat there. He's rang me since. It's been quite good, really."

She shares that she benefitted from conference because "I can say that I was there. That's mainly what I feel, that I was there. I met the family. I met some of the other people afterwards — some of the friends of Michael. ... I was quite happy to be involved because I thought even beforehand if ever I meet these people that I'd love to say, "I'm sorry. I'm sorry you lost your son. I'm sorry that my son was involved. "

Describing her son, Douglas, Joanne says, "It's about 15 years now since he's lived at home. We didn't even know where he was. So he's been here, there and everywhere ...

"He was a very hard boy to control. His father was very strict with him. And I've always felt that he was too strict. ... They didn't get on well at all. They used to clash all the time. And so his father told him to leave home, and he did. He had a very poor education. He never amounted to anything. He got in with the wrong sort of boys from time to time. ... So he's been doing crime on and off for a long time."

"And you have stuck by Douglas?"

"Yeah, well, there's a lot of good things about him. He's such a devil, but he's got something lovable about him. You know, you can't help it really, being a mum."

Brendon Dorff

Brendon Dorff, Michael's boyhood friend, explains that his "initial thoughts were, 'No way I'm going to do this.' ... [But later] I thought yes, maybe it would be a good idea to support those people, whether it be Joan or Ken or Sarah or whoever else. ... I didn't really have any expectations. I guess just meeting them and talking to them. I think that was the main thing, sitting down with them. I think I would have liked the answer to, 'Why?' ... But that didn't happen, unfortunately.

"The conference itself, I thought it was very good. ... It gave everyone an opportunity to speak. It gave an opportunity different from the courts where you hear all these wonderful things about the accused — or the guilty in this case, the murderers. You hear all these wonderful things like their personal character references and things like that. Now it was really a good opportunity for us to say how wonderful Michael was."

For Brendon, having his friend Michael Marslew acknowledged seems to have been the most conspicuous benefit of the conference.

O'Connell asks, "What could have given you more closure?"

He responds, "My big question was, 'Why was Michael killed?' I don't know. It wasn't answered. A few things would have been good to see: the other murderers there, like Vince Piller, involved in the conference, the person who actually shot the gun."

Brendon's perception that not "all that much has changed" for him is different than Joan Griffiths' perspective, expressed in her interview. She has known Brendon since he and her son were toddlers and she sees significant changes in Brendon after participating in the conference.

"Brendon never really wanted to acknowledge the fact that Michael was gone. He never liked to talk about it when he came around ... Since the conference, he actually came around and we've spoken about Michael's death for the first time since Michael was killed.

"I think there's a healing there, too. He seems to be getting on with his life. He's doing lots of stuff ... He's just got his [driver's] license. He's never got his license, you see."

Joan Griffiths

Joan, Michael's mother, says that at the outset she "had really serious doubts about whether I wanted to have anything to do with the process, probably because I didn't want the offenders to get anything out of it. ... The other big factor was Ken was involved in it, and I'm always filled with doubts with anything that Ken has any involvement in. ...

"The positive for me was the fact that I was going to be able to say to the offenders all the things that I hadn't been allowed to say up to that point. ... It might be a way I could tell them how much they'd hurt us and how the suffering is going to go on for everybody. ... I don't want them to just walk away and feel that they served their term and it's all over because it's never over for the people they've left behind."

Joan expresses her frustration with the criminal justice system's focus on offenders. She says, "You go through the court system, where you see them being looked after and feted, and they're given everything they possibly can be given. And you're just left out in the cold."

She anticipated that in the conference she wanted the offenders to realize "What they'd done to Michael, which I don't think had even dawned on them. You know, they killed someone and, 'So what?' What they'd done to not only me, but everybody else concerned with Michael. He was a very popular young man, not only in his family, but with friends and associates ... He was just that sort of person, very dynamic personality. ... They've robbed the family of Michael. They've robbed Michael's friends of all the help and love he used to give them.

"I wanted them to take responsibility, which they did. I was quite surprised. They did acknowledge the fact that they were responsible for his death. That was a relief for me because that was something I wanted from them. And that was good.

"Very draining. It took me a long time to get over it. It really wiped me out. Emotionally it was very, very difficult. Immediately after it, I'm talking about the same night, there was a great sense of relief. I'd unloaded all the garbage I'd been carrying around for years, all the things that had been eating me up that I hadn't been allowed to say. So there was this big relief. I've gotten it off my chest, and I felt really good."

As for the conference itself, Joan explains, "It was good. It flowed very, very well. Your convening did that. I wouldn't have known where to start if I'd have walked in on my own. ... Just asking the questions and putting some sort of order to what we wanted to say and organizing it like that. ... I think it was important that everybody got the chance to say something."

"I thought for the young people that were at the Pizza Hut with Michael ... having spoken to them since ... I think it took away a lot of the fear of the unknown. There were these people that one night were monsters that came into their lives and just destroyed their innocence and their friend and their trust. ... 'Facing the Demons' was right because that's what they'd been to them. But in the end, they were just two pathetic people. ... I think that's what they got out of it. I think it laid a lot of things to rest for them. I think maybe they've been able to get on with their life a little bit better now that they've gotten some of their anger out, too.

"I thought she [Joanne Edwards] was very brave, especially under the circumstances, because the other parents hadn't come. I thought it showed a lot of gumption. ... I felt a bit sorry for her. I must admit that's something I hadn't taken into account until the conference, the impact of what had happened on the parents of the perpetrators ... but she'd been hurt through no fault of her own, which was very sad.

"I think I function a lot better than I used to in just about everything. I've just been able to get on more with a normal life, which is all I ever wanted. ... Once I got the chance to tell them what I thought, then I just set about putting my life back on track again and doing the normal things that other people do and that I used to do before I lost my son.

"After Michael was killed, I couldn't remember a lot of the years before. I lost it. It was as if the whole of my life started the night Michael was killed, and I couldn't see anything before that. I had to rely on people that knew him in the family and would talk about things. And they'd say, 'Can't you remember such and such? ... It was just as if somebody had wiped the slate clean. I think it was all the awful thoughts that were in my head just blocked out all the nice things, you know.

"It wasn't just the fact that I lost the physical Michael, I'd lost all the emotional Michael, too — all the good bits that you want to remember. ... And I got that back. It's gradually come back. I can remember all those good bits, and that's made things much better for me because I've got 19 years of him now, whereas all I had was this really bad night.

"It's just like somebody had come through with a broom and swept away all the things that had been preying on my mind for four years. It allowed some of the good things to start seeping back in gradually. I don't know exactly how it happened. It just seemed to happen. The only thing I can pinpoint it to is the actual time of the conference. ... That seemed to be the turning point, and I think it's just been a gradual healing. Now I'm getting him back little by little, and it's lovely. It's good to have him back.

"It's a physical hurt when somebody's killed like this — or I think when you lose a child in any circumstances. ... You'll try anything to ease that hurt. ... I joined that support group, which wasn't for me.

... It tends to cultivate this grieving cycle and not encourage you to work through it. ... This is not what I want to do with my life. This means that this murder is going to kill me as well as Michael.

"I saw a psychologist for a long, long time. He got me to the point where I could function. He was quite supportive of me going to the conference ... if I thought it was going to help me. I have seen him since. And he was quite pleased with the outcome and how it had helped me."

Sarah Anderson

Before the conference Sarah Anderson, one of Michael's best friends, says, "I was scared, but not scared of them, seeing Douglas and Karl. It wasn't that so much. It was just that I had built up an idea about what they were like. It wasn't a bad picture. I thought that — I was hoping that they were going to be basically normal people like me and my friends and stuff, but who have just made a really bad judgment, a severe bad judgment, but nonetheless still good people. I was afraid that when I got to this thing that they would be really bad people. And my whole view of the world would change. That was probably the main thing.

"But I also was interested because I wanted to ask them what did they think about leading up to the robbery and then before Michael got killed and stuff. Just to find out — did they think? What thoughts went through their mind? Especially when I found out that Karl has a little son. I was like, 'Didn't you think about him? How would he feel if he found out that you did this, even if you got away with it?' It was just things like that that entered my mind.

"The first shock was going into the room. It was set up totally different to what I thought it was. I think it was having the criminals on one side and the people on the other side, separating it. Having a big table or something between us, you know. I just thought it for safety reasons — no one lunging across the room or something. But we were just in a circle to talk. And it made it sort of freaky in a way because it was just personal. It made it more personal, and that sort of feeling just ... it changed it because Karl was going to be sitting right there, and I'm like, 'I don't know about this. He's coming in my space.' Even though he wasn't in close proximity, it was still a personal feeling, a communal group feel to it. Sitting in a circle, everyone's involved.

"I liked how Terry O'Connell ran it, that we all got to say something. No one was ever interrupted. Everyone got to say how they felt, including Karl and Douglas. That was important.

"I remember asking Karl, 'What did you think? What were you thinking about? Did you plan like, what if this happens, what if that happens?' And he goes, 'No, we didn't. That was the point. We didn't think.' Just looking at him, and he spoke and he looked you in the eye, it was obvious that was exactly it — they just didn't think. All they wanted to do was get some money and get out.

"Just listening to them there, I sort of felt better because they were decent people. They just made a mistake. So what I was hoping they would be like turned out to be true. It made a total difference for me of how I viewed them. I didn't hate them. I don't pity them either ...

"I also got benefit afterwards. At the end of the conference we said all our things. Then I got a chance to talk to Karl just one-on-one. That was just after. I just got a chance to say, 'Hey, I'm not judging you. I'm not hating you. I don't blame you for the actual act of Michael dying because that was taken out of your hands [by Vincent Piller].'

"I've let go a lot of anger. That has probably been the best thing. All my anger towards Karl and Douglas, anyway, is gone. I don't have anger. I don't wish them ill will. Actually, I just hope that when they get out of jail, their life can be as normal as possible and that they can still function in society, especially with Karl being in jail for a long time.

"With me, it provided some closure to the whole episode. It doesn't bring Michael back, and I miss him. ... But it brings like, 'OK, you can't change it. However, it's time to move on.'

"With that, it supported my whole idea that these people are good people, they've just made a mistake. It supported my philosophy that most people in the world are nice and kind and generous.

But sometimes through pressure of situation of whatever — it's not an excuse, but sometimes some are just not as strong as others. And they do the wrong thing and take the wrong path. But I think second chances are important.

"All I can say really is that I think the conference was the healing point for me. It healed me and allowed me to sort of get my act together and actually start to function in the world again."

Shortly after the conference Sarah went on a trip to the United States and returned home and resumed her university studies to become a primary school teacher.

Karl Kramer Returns to Prison

Contrary to Sarah Anderson's and Ken Marslew's optimistic hopes, Karl Kramer failed to change. When he was released in 2009, Marslew met Kramer outside the prison. He had arranged for Kramer to assist with his anti-violence organization's work. At the time Marslew said, "I'm just hoping that something good will come out of this but only time will tell."[55] According to newspaper reports, Kramer committed a new offense "a mere seven weeks after his parole."[56] A few months later he was arrested again and returned to prison after "bursting in a home ... and attacking two men with a blue metal baseball bat."[57]

So if our expectations for restorative justice are confined to changing offender behavior, we may experience disappointment. But if our expectations focus on reducing the emotional impact of crime for victims, family and friends, the outcomes will be reliable and rewarding.

No Big Deal

We often judge the emotional impact of a crime by the severity of the offense, but lesser crimes often wreak havoc in people's lives, not because of physical harm but because the crime disrupts feelings of safety and normality.

Terry O'Connell told me a story while I was in Australia about the theft of a motor bike from the veranda of a suburban home. No big deal. Just a motor bike, not much expense, no violence. The family consisted of a mom and dad and four little girls who ranged in age from 4 to 12 years old.

Terry "rang" the mother on the telephone and asked if she wanted to participate in a restorative conference with the two teenage boys who had been apprehended and had admitted the offense. "No, we would be too terrified," she said. "I'm going to get counselors. My family has been severely traumatized."

Terry responded sympathetically. He asked if he could come and speak to the family personally, to explain how the conference might address that fear and trauma. The mother agreed, and after his visit the family eventually agreed to participate in a conference.

In the conference, the mother spoke emotionally to the boys, as did the oldest sister. Both spoke in general terms about how the theft had traumatized the younger sisters. Although they talked only in general terms in the conference, Terry later learned that the youngest sister, after the incident, started wetting her bed. Still another insisted on sleeping with her parents. The second oldest sister wouldn't go out on the back veranda after dark.

Because the motor bike was recovered, there was no financial restitution involved. The agreement focused on apologies and some community service work.

After the conference ended and the offenders left, O'Connell chatted with the family. The mother assured him that the conference had brought her family closure. She said that she had no idea how they would have effectively dealt with the aftermath of this event without the conference. The 12-year-old began to cry, with her younger sisters watching her. "I felt really sorry for those two boys," she exclaimed. "They're just like the boys down the road." For she and her sisters the face-to-face meeting with the boys made the offenders real and normal, removing the fear from their nights.

When Terry followed up a week later, the mother said that the conference had been a fabulous experience for the family. The girls had not stopped talking about it. The youngest girl stopped wetting her bed, the next youngest no longer needed to sleep with her parents, and the second oldest once again felt safe on the back veranda after dark. The issues of trauma had not surfaced again and the family's life had returned to normal.[58]

Evidence

In 2007 a comprehensive review of research in the United Kingdom and other countries, conducted under the auspices of the Smith Institute, showed that restorative justice (the research dealt primarily with restorative conferences, not victim-offender mediation):

> - substantially reduced repeat offending for some offenders, but not all;
> - doubled (or more) the offences brought to justice as diversion from the current system;
> - reduced crime victims' post-traumatic stress symptoms and related costs;
> - provided both victims and offenders with more satisfaction with justice than the current system;
> - reduced crime victims' desire for violent revenge against their offenders;
> - reduced the costs of criminal justice, when used as diversion from the current system;
> - reduced recidivism more than prison (adults) or as well as prison (youths).[59]

On the other hand, in 2012 an Australian research study that compared re-offending rates between young offenders who went to court versus those who went through restorative "youth justice conferences" in New South Wales did not show that conferencing was preferable to court. The contrary findings may be due to the quality of the conferences. However, the two Australian researchers also challenged the 2007 Smith Institute review, arguing that "the studies reviewed provide little basis for confidence that conferencing reduces re-offending at all."[60]

While there is obviously some dispute, the British review was more comprehensive. Nonetheless, there is strong and uncontested evidence that restorative conferences *reduce the negative impact of crime*. That alone provides sufficient justification for making "reduction of harm" a fundamental goal of our criminal justice systems. The 2007 Smith Institute review of conferencing research concurs: "On the grounds of helping victims for the intrinsic merit of that goal, the evidence for RJ is compelling."[61]

Perhaps the most exciting research results dealt with post-traumatic stress disorder, which often persists for years after an incident of crime has taken place. Dr. Caroline Angel, at the University of Pennsylvania, studied the effects of restorative conferences on burglary and robbery victims. She states, "The most striking thing was that conferences reduced symptoms of post-traumatic stress disorder. What you have here is a one-time program that's effective in producing benefits for the majority of people."[62]

"They're just like the boys down the road"

Those words of the 12-year-old girl whose family's motor bike was stolen from the porch of their home in Australia illustrate how a restorative justice conference can normalize relationships and thereby ease fears and feelings. Like Michael Marslew's family and friends, the four young sisters had an opportunity to "face the demons." Similarly, after more than four years of trauma, Brendon Dorff now was able to talk with Michael's parents about their son's death, and he finally obtained his driver's license. Sarah Anderson went on a trip to America and resumed her university studies. Joan Griffiths functioned "a lot better in just about everything" and recovered a lifetime of memories of Michael, lost after seeing him in the morgue.

Conferences may be convened at any point in the criminal justice process. Diverting young offenders from the court, as happened with the motor bike theft, or before offenders are sentenced so that victims and families might have a say in what should happen, or during incarceration as depicted in "Facing the Demons," or as part of an offender's release process, facilitating the offender's return to his or her home community.

Karl Kramer, of course, is a disappointment to those who hoped he might change. Despite his articulate expression of concern and his thoughtful insights about himself and others, he still reverted to his worst behaviors — impulsivity and aggression — possibly exacerbated by substance abuse. Many young people in our CSF Buxmont schools and group homes have those same issues. Perhaps it's not realistic to expect a single restorative event to change all that. However, the success of the CSF Buxmont restorative milieu in changing student behavior — through restorative encounters repeated day after day — suggests that perhaps our prisons should also be run as restorative milieus.

Whether or not conferencing reliably reduces re-offending, restorative conferences achieve real justice for victims and others harmed by crime. Is there a better goal for the criminal justice system? We may not always change offender behavior, but from the least to the most serious crimes, we can provide those harmed with a way to face their demons and mitigate their trauma.

Family Power

Chapter 5
Family Power[63]

When New Zealand passed a new Children, Young Persons and Their Families Act in 1989, no one could have predicted the revolutionary impact it would have around the world — in social work initially, but ultimately in related fields. The law granted families, whose children might otherwise be removed from their homes, the right to meet and develop an alternative plan before such an action is taken. The legislation created a process to make this possible and named it a "family group conference" or FGC, which has spread around the world. In North America it later acquired the name "family group decision making" or FGDM.

The most radical feature of this law is its requirement that — after social workers and other professionals brief the family on the government's expectations and the services and resources available to support their plan — the professionals must leave the room. This "family alone time" or "family private time" is when the extended family and friends of the family have an opportunity to take responsibility for their own loved ones. Never before in the history of the modern interventionist state has a government shown so much respect for the rights and potential strengths of families.

I remember attending a professional conference about FGC in England where I heard a grandmother describe how terrified she had been that social workers were going to place her grandchildren in foster care because her daughter, a single mother, suffered severe depression. The grandmother poignantly described her family's feelings of helplessness and desperation in the face of the power of government, however well-intentioned, to swoop into their lives and take away the children that they loved so dearly.

I gained a deeply emotional insight into how the skies suddenly brightened when the grandmother and her extended family were offered an opportunity to participate in a family group conference. Grandparents and aunts and uncles all rallied around the struggling mother. They created a structured schedule of visitation and volunteer support at critical hours of the day that ensured the well-being of her children. The plan was sufficiently rigorous to satisfy the concerns that had brought about the threatened intervention by government. Not only did it fulfill the needs of the children, but mobilizing the extended family's involvement saved the government considerable expense.

Since the advent of FGC in New Zealand, instead of a social worker unilaterally making a recommendation to the court, a conference coordinator is assigned to help organize a family conference and frame the discussion. The coordinator assists the family in determining who to include in the conference and prepares the conference participants by explaining what to expect and answering questions about the process. The coordinator also prepares support people to be there for the family and coordinates the availability of professionals. The professionals come to the conference to explain relevant legal requirements, the safety issues and other specific concerns for the family and child that need to be addressed during the meeting, as well as any other information about available resources that might help the family make the best possible plan.

Once the professionals have prepared the family for the conference, the family group meets privately to develop their own plan. Only at the conclusion of the private meeting are the professionals invited back into the room to hear a presentation of the family's plan. So long as the family plan meets all the basic expectations and legal parameters laid out by the professionals before the conference, the social worker and the family court recognize it as the official service plan. The social worker then helps the family carry out the plan and monitors its progress.

Bold yet simple, the law turned the existing assumptions of the social work field upside down. New Zealand's groundbreaking legislation represented a new way of thinking, a paradigm shift for people in the helping professions.

The old paradigm, while well-intentioned, embodied an attitude of "we know better." It assumed that people needed help from the outside. It assumed that a child in tough circumstances would be better served by government intervention and by being removed from his or her family and community. It assumed that social workers had the answers for the family. Based on these assumptions, the old paradigm placed most of the power in the hands of professionals.

But the new thinking, which we call restorative practices, and the FGC process itself, embodies the values of respect, collaboration, shared responsibility and accountability. The new premise assumes that professionals are there to support families so that families can help themselves. A social worker's job is no longer to solve problems for families but to engage in fruitful dialog and to support change. Decision-making and action remain largely with families themselves — in recognition of a family's own power.

The idea of the FGC sprang from the social welfare and child protection services field. But the idea of working *with* people, rather than doing things *for* them or *to* them, has implications for anyone who works with young people and families, including teachers and school administrators, social service providers, alternative school counselors and staff, police, probation officers and corrections officers, foster care providers and family counselors. There are even implications for the medical field and care of the elderly.

Families in Crisis

When a child is abused or neglected, when a teenager gets arrested, becomes violent toward his or her parents and family or has spun out of control with alcohol or other drugs, when a parent is sentenced to prison or sent to a drug rehabilitation center, when domestic violence occurs and recurs — government steps in to oversee and assume responsibility. Frequently that means removing young people from their homes and placing them in other homes or facilities that government and its professional staff regard as safe and therapeutic.

For the family and the child, this can be a terrible blow. When a situation gets so bad that the government intervenes, the family is already experiencing a great deal of stress and chaos. When others outside the family are making serious decisions that affect the integrity of the family, the impact can be truly devastating.

Family members may feel frustrated, ignored, helpless and disempowered. They may believe that they neither have the means nor the right to ask questions, or they may be too afraid to ask questions for fear of repercussion. In truth, sometimes government does make bad decisions that adversely affect innocent families, which is no surprise, given human fallibility combined with the strong powers granted to government agencies. However, in the vast majority of cases where someone in a family has violated laws or compromised the well-being of children, intervention by a government agency is justified and necessary.

How can government interventions become more effective? How can social workers, educators and other professionals overcome family members' shame and other obstacles and achieve a connection with families so progress can be made? What does it mean to empower families, given the sometimes adversarial relationships that develop between them and the professionals? What does family engagement look like? How can the collaborative process between professionals and clients begin? How can this more meaningful way of working with families be employed? What would be the result if everyone upheld the values of family empowerment? The following stories address these questions and illustrate the wide variety of cases where a restorative approach — formal FGC/FGDM conferences — can be used effectively.

Rebecca's Story

Rebecca, a 15-year-old girl, left home to live with the family of a friend. She was not a runaway. Rather, the purpose of her temporary move was, in part, to relieve tension between her and her mother. This was a private arrangement made between the two families. There had been no social welfare agency involvement, although Rebecca did have a relationship with a home visitor from her school.

When the time came for Rebecca to move back home, however, she refused to go. Instead, she reported that her mother was a raging alcoholic, and at this point the local county children and youth service agency became involved in the case.

When a child has been separated from his or her primary family, the goal of social services is to reunify the family. However, concerns for the protection of the child can be an obstacle to achieving this goal. In Rebecca's situation, her mother's alcoholism was the primary concern. An FGC/FGDM gives extended family and close supporters an opportunity to meet and develop a plan to satisfy safety concerns and other requirements so that a child can be reunited with family. When reunification with immediate family is ultimately not possible, many families use the FGC/FGDM process to find a place for a child within the extended family. Failing that, they may also develop visitation and other plans for family members to communicate and stay connected with children, even when the child lives in long-term foster care or some other residential placement.

Rebecca's caseworker believed an FGC/FGDM might be the best way for her and her mother to come together, with the support of extended family, to create a reunification plan. Rebecca's case was assigned to a non-profit agency that had a contract with the government to provide FGC/FGDM coordinators but was independent and impartial.

Once the coordinator learns the particulars of the case, she typically begins by meeting together with the nuclear family. In this situation, she met separately with Rebecca and her mother to explain the conference process, obtain their consent and begin the planning process. The coordinator reviewed the concerns that the referring social worker has said needed to be addressed during the FGC/FGDM. These so-called "bottom lines" are those issues that must be addressed by the conference plan in order for the plan to be acceptable to the caseworker and ultimately the family court. The coordinator explains the FGC/FGDM process, including the fact that the family will meet privately to develop their own plan, which, if approved, becomes the service plan for the case. If the family agrees to participate in the process, the coordinator ask them which other family members and closely family friends would be available to support the nuclear family and help make the plan.

A coordinator always seeks to create the widest circle of participants possible and urges the immediate family not to exclude anyone simply because they fear that certain people either would not want to come or should not come for whatever reason. From experience we know that the more people who are included, the more likely they are to develop a strong, common-sense plan. The more voices there are, the more normative the effect, the more stable the group, and the more talent, knowledge, creativity and support is available.

Rebecca's father was not invited to the conference. While coordinators usually reach out to fathers and their families, Rebecca's father had always been completely absent from her life.

Unfortunately, Rebecca's mother had burned bridges with many on her own side of the family. Nonetheless, several of Rebecca's family members on her mother's side did agree to attend the conference, including Rebecca's aunt and uncle (her mother's sister and brother-in-law) and her grandparents. Rebecca's stepfather and 10-year-old younger brother also came. A very close longtime friend of Rebecca's mother also attended. The parents of the friend where Rebecca was staying were invited to participate. They were not able to attend but wrote a letter of support to be read at the conference.

Ultimately, only eight participants attended the FGC/FGDM conference, fewer than the average of 12 to 15 participants. Some coordinators will not hold a conference with fewer than five attendees because the formal structure tends to make a smaller number of people feel uncomfortable. In such situations, the coordinator may opt to hold a more informal circle instead, as described later in this book.

Children are welcome and encouraged to attend and participate in the FGC/FGDM conference, although their participation may be limited depending on the circumstances of the case. School-age children and teenagers like Rebecca, who can articulate their feelings about what is happening in the family, usually participate as full members of the conference. Even younger children may be given a chance to offer their opinions and thoughts. The presence of infants and toddlers serves as a reminder to everyone else that children are at the center of the process and that their welfare is what the conference is all about.

When inviting participants, a coordinator should not only phone people, but, if possible, visit in person with every potential conference participant. An in-person visit improves the personal connection and relationship building, ensures that everyone understands the process and helps the coordinator foresee and address possible problems and concerns that may arise during the FGC/FGDM. During these personal visits, the coordinator may also uncover other issues that ought to be considered in order for the family to make a good plan with the best chance of success.

The entire planning process, which usually extends over several weeks, helps make the FGC/FGDM more than a one-time meeting. It is an ongoing process that focuses on building relationships, fostering supportive connections and problem solving. While the eventual outcome may or may not be what the professionals had envisioned, the respectful solution-oriented approach adopted by the coordinator helps families move in a positive direction, and often they come up with effective plans that never would have occurred to the professionals.

Besides family members and a close friend of the family, several professionals were also invited to Rebecca's conference. These included Rebecca's counselor and the home visitor from the school, both of whom had good relationships with Rebecca and were very involved and available to support the family. The social worker from the local office of children and youth services who referred the case also attended, along with a SCOH (Services to Children in their Own Homes) worker.

The professionals are involved only during the initial "information sharing" phase of the conference. Once they have presented all the relevant information and answered questions — in a relatively short period of time so there is plenty of time for the rest of the conference — the professionals leave the room and allow the family to meet privately. If possible, they remain nearby in case the family has further questions or needs clarification and to be available when the family is ready to present their plan. However, the professionals are specifically instructed not to speak or gossip about the family or the conference while they are waiting.

The primary concern of the office of children and youth services was Rebecca's mother's alcohol abuse. The referring worker stipulated a "bottom line" in advance, which was that before Rebecca returned home, her mother needed to come up with a plan to attend individual counseling and therapy sessions in addition to Alcoholics Anonymous meetings. On a more general level, the focus of the conference had to do with helping Rebecca and her mother establish a more trusting relationship.

During family private time, the participants sorted through the issues noted above and drew up a plan to gradually transition Rebecca from living with her friend's family to living at home. Because the professionals — including the conference coordinator — were not present during this phase, the actual course of discussion is unknown. The coordinator reported that, judging from the outcomes and from participants' comments afterward, one of the key issues addressed during the conference was the relationship between Rebecca's mother and her mother's sister, Rebecca's aunt. The mother said that she often felt undermined by Rebecca's aunt, who said things to Rebecca that contradicted her mother's decisions and her authority. The resulting plan stipulated that the aunt would limit her phone calls with Rebecca and that she would allow Rebecca's mother's therapist to deal with those issues she might otherwise have raised.

In another part of their plan, Rebecca and her mother agreed to have lunch together once a week to work on their relationship. These meetings would help them prepare for and decide when it would be time for Rebecca to move back home.

In addition, Rebecca made plans to develop her relationship with her stepfather. She also agreed to "not spit, hit or tackle" her brother when he asked her to do things for him. This specific agreement was undoubtedly in response to concerns he voiced during the conference.

There are many ways to measure the success of a conference. Participant satisfaction is one method. The extent to which a family carries out their plan is another. The FGC/FGDM is more than a singular event. It is also a conversation starter, relationship builder and problem-solving mechanism. As such, the event produces qualitative results that can be hard to measure but which are apparent to those in the family or others involved in the conference.

In Rebecca's situation, she was reunited with her mother within two months of the initial conference. The coordinator credits Rebecca's counselor and school home visit worker for doing much to support the family to reach their goal. A follow-up conference shortly after Rebecca returned home revealed that the family still had some unresolved issues. During this meeting, Rebecca's brother articulated that he felt left out because of all the attention devoted to Rebecca during this crisis, so the family made further plans to address his needs. At this meeting, Rebecca also made a commitment to attend Alateen meetings (support groups for teenage children with an alcoholic parent or significant loved one) to learn how to cope with the effects of her mother's alcoholism.

Baby John's Story

Other than small variations from one locale or jurisdiction to another, the structure of the FGC/FGDM is consistent. But the details of every FGC/FGDM are different. That's what makes this type of conference such a useful tool. Each family can craft a plan that suits its own needs and circumstances.

In another FGC/FGDM case, a mother had to give up John, her newborn child, to foster care because she tested positive for heroin and marijuana during the delivery. She was offered an opportunity to be involved in an FGC/FGDM. She agreed at first but later refused. However, John's father, from whom the mother estranged herself shortly after the birth, took advantage of the opportunity and attended the FGC/FGDM that had been convened to plan for how the family could care for John. With the assistance and support of his parents, he and the family crafted a plan.

John would live with his paternal grandparents temporarily until his father could successfully complete the substance abuse treatment program he was in and move out of a halfway house. John's father would then live at home with his parents and John and attempt to regain legal custody of his baby boy. The young man followed through with this plan and was successful in his appeal. During the court hearing, in which he was granted custody of John, the court acknowledged that the father's participation in an FGC/FGDM had been a deciding factor. John's mother was granted visitation rights, but only on the condition that she not breach certain guidelines. Since she had refused to participate in the conference, children and youth services and the court made these decisions for her.

George and Sarah's Story

Gale Burford and Joan Pennell were the principal investigators for a conferencing project in Newfoundland and Labrador, Canada, which dealt with cases of domestic violence between the adults in families. At the time they were both professors of social work at Memorial University of Newfoundland. They used the term family group decision making (FGDM), which has become the prevailing term for family group conferences in North America. They reported the following as one of the case studies from the project.[64]

George, the husband, was due to be released from prison for violence against his wife, Sarah. Their two young sons, Kevin and Jason, had witnessed the violence. Sarah wanted a conference, even though she did not want to take George back. However, she was not certain she would stick to her resolve, having taken him back many times in the past when she had not intended to do so.

The conference was very challenging for the coordinator. The couple's respective families needed a lot of preparation and explanation.

They were worried about getting involved again in the couple's conflicts and that the conference would lapse into the patterns of the past, including mutual recrimination. George's family was quite large and had a long history of abuse and violence from living with a chronically alcoholic father. The coordinator took care to have the families discuss their views in advance. She was surprised at the candid revelations of George's mother, who would be likely to defend her son in public at the conference. But privately his mother acknowledged that he was very much like his father and admitted the negative impact his father's violence had on the whole family.

Meeting with George to prepare him for the conference was a special challenge because the coordinator had to navigate the bureaucracy of the penal and correctional systems. George was also reluctant to participate at first, fearing that everyone would pick on him and gossip about his personal business. His son Kevin was terrified of his father and chose not to attend in person but wrote out a statement, which was read aloud at the conference.

Bringing together all of these people raises understandable fears that the process would endanger participants during and after the conference. Coordinators who handle domestic abuse conferences must be knowledgeable and experienced in order to appropriately address these issues.

George and Sarah's conference began in the morning with the coordinator setting clear ground rules for confidentiality, listening to each other and remaining nonviolent. She reiterated the focus of the conference: ensuring the future safety of all family members and maximizing George's chances for rehabilitation.

The parole officer reported what had happened in the family and what concerns needed to be addressed, and then he explained parole

and what services he could offer. He found both families very atten-
tive because family members usually are not provided with that kind
of information. The conference participants were similarly impressed
with the representative from the women's shelter, who explained the
effects of violence and addiction on women and children. George's
mother commented that she wished such services had been available
to her years ago.

The coordinator read aloud Kevin's statement, which reduced
George to tears. As a result of Kevin's letter, George's family stopped
blaming Sarah for having turned him in to the police and agreed that
no child should be so frightened. What most amazed the parole officer was that George's father came to the conference.

During breaks and lunch, the parole officer chatted informally
with family members and was able to explain how "ratting" on
George to him would actually help George. Later during private time,
the families put "reporting on George" into the plan, and George
agreed to it. By mid-afternoon a good plan had been proposed and
approved. It included a safety plan for Sarah, visitation by the sons
with their father at the correctional center, counseling for Sarah and
Kevin and addictions counseling for George. The plan also specified
that if George, after his prison discharge, made unexpected visits to
Sarah, she would call his brothers and sisters, who would assist her
by making sure he left the premises. George agreed to all of this and
accepted that his family would no longer cover up for him.

The families were satisfied with the conference and cautiously
optimistic. As for the plan, it was largely followed, although it was
affected by the fact that George was not granted parole as quickly
as expected and stayed in prison a year longer. But George phoned
Sarah and the children regularly. Kevin was no longer frightened by
George, but he still worried about his mother's future safety. Sarah
went back to school, was seeing a counselor and was demonstrating
confidence and a sense of empowerment.

When George was finally discharged, Sarah subsequently
reported that they were getting along better. Despite the fact that

she had a rift with his family (unrelated to the conference), so that she could not call on them when George came over unannounced, she reported that this was not a problem and that she was no longer afraid of him. In general, she felt that getting things out in the open had made a great deal of difference.

Eric's Story

CSF and Buxmont, the IIRP's sister agencies, work in tandem to serve delinquent and at-risk youth in eastern Pennsylvania. They use the FGC/FGDM process routinely when youth are about to be discharged from foster care and school programs and return home. FGC/FGDM is offered as a voluntary option for young people and their families to develop transition plans so that habits learned in the more controlled environment of the foster homes can be sustained by youth back in their homes, communities, public schools and workplaces.

Eric was discharged from the residential program but did not have a home to which he could return. Upon graduating from high school, he was planning to move into an independent living program as he transitioned to being a young adult in the community. While he wouldn't be able to live with them, he did have extended family members who wanted to be involved in his life and were supportive of his goals.

So an FGC/FGDM was held to celebrate the young man's successful graduation and completion of the foster care program and to make a family support plan. His grandmother, aunt and several other relatives attended the conference and offered various kinds of help. One said, "I'll see him on weekends." Another said, "He can do his laundry at my house." A third family member said that they would take him to church. The director of the foster care program took the show of support by family to indicate that the young man would "fall back into a great safety net." This story also illustrates that conferences can be held in situations that don't necessarily constitute a crisis. The FGC/FGDM can celebrate a positive occasion and proactively create family engagement that might not occur without organizing a meeting for everyone who cares about the young person.

Similarly, probation departments and social services agencies have referred youth and adults to FGC/FGDM to develop plans to help them transition from detention facilities, drug rehabilitation programs and other facilities back to their homes or other community placements.

János' Story

Vidia Negrea, director of the Community Service Foundation in Hungary, a non-profit affiliate of the IIRP based in Budapest, has done work in prisons. She organized an FGC/FGDM for a man named János, who, after more than a decade of imprisonment for second-degree murder, awaited release back into his community. His prison warden learned about conferencing and referred him to Negrea. János was chosen for his good behavior and because he had maintained a relationship with his family.

Negrea first went to the home of János' family and met his partner, their two children and his partner's parents, in whose house they all lived during János' imprisonment. This preliminary meeting constituted the planning stage for an informal family meeting with prison staff — not a formal conference, which would come later — to plan a Christmas furlough for János. The furlough would allow everyone to test the waters and help János transition to a full parole within the year.

All parties deemed János' home visit successful so Negrea proceeded to plan a formal FGC/FGDM. The primary purpose of the conference was to help János in his efforts to return from prison with the support and resources to become a law-abiding citizen and successful family and community member. In the preliminary informal meeting, the family and prison staff had identified a key question: How would they build community support for János? Everyone anticipated that news of a convicted murderer coming home might spread through town and stir up anxieties. They hoped to prevent prejudice against János so that he could achieve acceptance. Other conference goals included helping János find a good job so that he could pay back his debts and make reparations to the family of his victim.

Eight family members, six professionals and three supporters (the village chaplain, his wife and a psychology student who worked with János) attended the FGC/FGDM. János began the conference by introducing key discussion issues and presenting his plans and major concerns. The professionals discussed resources for finding a job and supporting the family, as well as community social services for him and his family. During family alone time, the family developed a specific plan about where János and his immediate family would live, where János would work and how he would pay his debts, maintain positive relationships and make reparations to his family, the community and the relatives of the victim. The professionals approved the plan and agreed that, should János breach the conditions of his release, he would face serious consequences, including returning to prison to complete his sentence and losing his family's support. Fortunately, János was successful in following the plan.

Evidence

A review of research by the American Humane Association reported positive outcomes for using FGDM in child protection:

> In summary, the collective research showed that, when compared to traditional child welfare practices, child safety plans developed collaboratively by families, their support networks, and child welfare system representative are more likely to:
> > keep children safe
> > result in more permanent placements
> > decrease the need for foster care
> > maintain family bonds
> > increase family well-being

FGDM can be used to create effective solutions for even the most challenging child welfare situations. FGDM can be used successfully in situations of:

> neglect
> domestic violence
> substance abuse
> sexual and physical abuse

FGDM can be used regardless of factors such as:

> age
> race
> ethnicity
> and level of involvement in the child welfare system.[65]

A similar review undertaken for the government of Scotland was supportive but more cautious. It found that "FGC is expected to be effective in two ways: enabling the wider family to be fully involved in decision-making and planning for children and achieving better outcomes for children."[66]

The executive report of the review concluded that "FGC was viewed as an ethically sound and practically effective way of working with families whose strengths and resources often remain untapped by mainstream practice. ... There is however strong agreement, across the literature and those interviewed, that FGC is not a magic formula, but will only deliver improvements to services for children if it is offered as part of well-resourced core services." As for saving money, "The available evidence indicates that FGC is likely to be cost neutral or to provide savings." I suspect that the latter somewhat ambivalent finding is due to the varied quality of FGC in different jurisdictions.

Where the conferences are of consistently high quality, the results are more compelling. Eigen Kracht, a Dutch non-profit organization, is a world leader in conferencing that has developed a reliable and cost-effective approach — using non-professionals trained as coordinators and paid on a per-conference basis:

Research shows that Eigen Kracht conferences are effective, even in complex situations where youth care is involved, in cases of domestic violence, as well where so-called multi-problem families are concerned. The costs are relatively low, clients are satisfied and in most cases the quality of the plan that families make is good, according to families as well as professionals. Most plans are executed, the problems are solved and escalation is prevented. In many cases, Eigen Kracht is effective as well as cost saving. This is because families use their own resources; instead of applying for residential care, as professionals might do, they arrange for help at home and for foster care instead of residential youth care. [67]

In a cost analysis of a range of cases, from residential care, foster care and non-residential cases, an Eigen Kracht conference dramatically reduces the cost of services. The "per file" cost of services averaged €8900 (euros), including the cost of the conference itself, in cases handled through Eigen Kracht. Comparable cases handled without an FGC averaged €16,180 in services provided per case — almost twice as much.[68]

Helping Families Help Themselves

The family is a robust institution that has been around as long as there have been human beings. Yet in a rapidly changing and increasingly complex world, families face difficult challenges and crises. In many places governments intervene in the problems of troubled families. But there are limits to what government can do. Of course, there are financial limitations, but there are also limitations inherent in the roles that professionals can play. They reach those limits when they try to do things *to* families and *for* families.

The best results are achieved through restorative practices, such as family group conferences, which help families help themselves. Professionals can engage and collaborate — doing things *with* families. They can provide information and access to resources. They can teach skills and help families communicate better. They can motivate nuclear families to reach out to their extended families and friends and support them in finding their own solutions. For we have come to realize that what benefits people the most is when they can rely upon their own family power.

Good Company

Chapter 6
Good Company

Toxic Talk[69]

"I'd like to welcome everyone coming here today. My name is Judy Happ and I'm going to be facilitating this conference."

Judy was following the restorative conference script that the IIRP's Real Justice program uses and shares with its trainees around the world. The script provides a structured sequence for providing a successful encounter between wrongdoers, those they have wronged and supporters for both of the respective parties. In this case it was a workplace conference.

She continued, "The conference focuses on a specific incident, although there have been other issues. ... And I've explained to everyone, this conference is going to focus on an incident that happened on a fishing trip, where people were talking behind Glenna's back. It's really important that people understand that we're going to focus on what people did and how that unacceptable behavior has affected other people.

"We're not here to decide whether anyone is good or bad. We're going to explore in what way people have been affected and hopefully work toward repairing the harm that's resulted."

She looked up at a staff member who was on the fishing trip. "Rich, would you tell us what happened?" And so the restorative conference began.

A few days earlier I and my fellow administrators in the CSF Buxmont organization learned that some of our staff had been publicly mocking and backstabbing their supervisor on the annual fishing trip organized by county juvenile probation officers who refer delinquent youth to our CSF Buxmont programs. They are our organization's customers. We thought about whether we had the right to address the issue because it occurred over the weekend, on our staff's own personal time. But the fact that the incident had reached our ears and that it had played out in such a public way made it clear that it was not a private matter. Rather, it was an organizational issue with significant negative implications for our agency.

Ironically, one of the last people to find out about the incident was Glenna, the young woman who had been the object of ridicule. She had recently been promoted to a supervisor position from among the ranks of her peers. She had made some minor mistakes in her new role, but she had repeatedly encouraged her former colleagues to tell her whenever they had concerns about her actions. Instead, they rewarded her humility and openness by criticizing and ridiculing her during at a public event.

Glenna was devastated when she heard about her humiliation at the hands of her former peers. But she reacted favorably to the idea of a restorative conference. Judy Happ, the executive director of the organization, volunteered to run the restorative conference and asked Glenna who she might want to attend as her supporters. She named her supervisor, Jim, and other administrators. Judy also invited others who had been impacted by the turmoil created in their workplace.

When confronted, the young employees admitted to the incident and reluctantly agreed to participate, understandably feeling uncomfortable about facing Glenna and others in such a public forum. To proceed with a restorative conference, wrongdoers must at least admit to their inappropriate actions or there is not much point in bringing everyone together. Unlike adversarial court processes, offenders in a restorative process are encouraged to take responsibility and invite others to attend who can provide them with emotional support.

In criminal justice settings we would recommend that offenders and, of course, victims only participate on a voluntary basis. However in our workplace setting, unlike in the larger community, everyone was going to have to face each other every day — so only the victim had a choice. Because everyone is paid to work in our agency and the emotional well-being of the organization is critical, a refusal by one of the wrongdoers would have called into question the likelihood of their continued employment.

The conference did not occur in isolation, as a singular event, but was part of a routinely supportive workplace environment where staff could confront their bosses with their concerns, where feedback and evaluation flowed both ways between staff and management on an ongoing basis, not just through formal annual evaluations. The context of the workplace significantly reduced the power imbalance issues that might have made the conference an overwhelming experience for young staff.

We decided that we were going to videotape the entire conference, again only asking the victim for her permission. For everyone else, we simply promised that, after the fact, we would edit out anyone who did not want to appear in the final product, a film eventually entitled *Toxic Talk: From Betrayal to Trust in the Workplace*. The film has provided viewers with a rare opportunity to learn the value of a restorative conference in a workplace setting.[70]

In the beginning of the conference, the wrongdoers were hesitant and somewhat defensive. At first, they responded to the restorative questions that Judy asked them in a way that minimized their responsibility, showed little empathy for Glenna and demonstrated concern mostly for themselves and their own feelings.

As the story unfolded it became apparent the precipitating issue on the day of the fishing trip was a leadership decision that staff from the "Supervision Program" were going to be required to attend the CSF Buxmont school graduations of their clients that same day. Some of them had planned to leave for the seashore early and now would not get there until later in the day.

Rich began: "Me, personally, I had some problems with the graduation and how it was put out. I guess I interpreted it as not being a directive. In that case, if I'm able to make it — great. If I'm not able to make it — then OK.

"And so on Thursday, it seemed to be more of a directive. And we should, as representatives of CSF Supervision, be at one of the graduations. It was at that point that we tried to work together a little bit and make sure we had representatives there.

"But going down to the shore on Friday, a lot of people were venting a lot of frustrations."

Judy asked, "Who do you think has been affected?"

Rich replied, "I think, definitely, Supervision [staff] as a whole. The people on the fishing trip were affected directly. I think other people throughout Supervision."

"In what ways? How do you think people have been affected?"

"Betrayal, unfortunately. Mistrust, of course. Basically, I think it made a lot of people feel uncomfortable right now. ...

"I was frustrated about the whole graduation thing, simply because I had never been to a graduation before. ... And I had always thought it was optional, because that was the way it was put out. I was just frustrated and felt like I hadn't been heard. And just ... angry."

Another staff member said, "So we all started just bitching. And Glenna was the focus because she was the one who put out [the announcement]. Because she's the coordinator, she put it out. So she was the focus. So there was someone to pinpoint all the problems on. So that's what we did.

"And I said some nasty, mean things that I'm not proud of."

Judy worked her way around the circle asking other wrongdoers the restorative questions.

"Who do you think has been affected by this incident?"

"Everybody, I think, in the organization, to some extent. It's pretty obvious there's something going on. Basically, everybody in this room has probably been affected. And I've been affected. I feel like I affected a lot of people. I know Shaun's affected. I know the other probation officers are aware that something's going on. And I'm sure the kids even know that something's not quite right. Especially with group last night, when everybody was just kind of ... skittish."

"I just feel like now, nobody's going to talk to anybody about anything. It's just going to be closed-mouthed, nobody's going to say a word. I don't think there's going to be any more trips. ... I personally had a great time. And I'm a little disappointed because now I don't want to go next year."

Then one of the wrongdoers shifted the group toward taking responsibility for what had been done to Glenna.

He said, "Not only did I feed into the negativity down there, but I saw it coming months ago. And I didn't step in and really take any action to prevent that from happening. I think the fishing trip and the incident on Friday just acted as a huge catalyst. And it afforded everyone an excuse, or an opportunity, to vent and to look for a scapegoat and basically place blame on Glenna. ... I took part in that, and I shouldn't have."

"Glenna, would you tell us what your reaction was when you first heard about the incident on Friday?"

She looked directly at those who had ridiculed her: "I found out visually when I walked into Williamson's on Tuesday and I looked around. I looked at every one of you and you guys couldn't even look me in the eye. And I knew right then and there that there was something wrong. ... And then I got a phone call from Barb, saying she needed to talk to me about some things ...

"And then [later] I called Jim [and told him] I want to quit. I don't want to work here anymore. How could these people do this? There's a process that needs to be followed. Some of you didn't follow that process ... if you had a problem. You didn't.

"Disgusting, sick. I didn't eat Tuesday, Wednesday. The first time I ate was today."

"What's been the hardest thing for you since you heard about it?"

"That I failed Jim [her supervisor] because people didn't get to me. And that makes me sick to my stomach."

"How did family and friends react when you talked to them?"

"I said to my husband Tuesday night — I told him everything I knew at that point. And he's like, 'Glenna, you're in a supervisory position. Things like this happen.'" But she insisted, "They shouldn't have happened."

One of her supervisors described Glenna on the day she had to confront her staff with the fact that they were expected to attend their clients' graduation before they left for their fishing trip.

"Glenna kept coming into my office that day. She was letting each of you know you needed to be at graduation. Asking me if I thought that she had handled it well, had she hurt anybody's feelings, so on and so forth. And that's the Glenna that I know. She's most concerned when she's confronting things that she needs to in her position, about hurting other people's feelings. And then I hear that people go behind her back and do nothing but hurt her feelings.

"It makes me angry. It makes me feel that people, I guess, don't get the concept of what this organization's about. This organization is about teamwork. It's about working together. It's about if you have a grievance, there is a process. People know they need to bring up their issues with other people in this agency, even though sometimes it's real difficult.

"And I think it was just a lot of people being cowards. It's what I think. And just being this dysfunctional, disgusting thing. The other thing that comes up for me is … I was in the same position as Glenna five years ago, when I became a coordinator. And I feel for you, Glenna. It really sucks to be in that position. Especially knowing how hard Glenna's trying to work to try to make the team together and seamless and everything that goes along with it."

For myself, as a founder of the CSF Buxmont programs, I have something of an "emeritus" role because I was no longer involved in the day-to-day operations, but focused on building the IIRP Graduate School. I participated in the circle because I was very much affected by what happened to Glenna, which was in total contradiction of the spirit of the organizational culture we have tried to build and maintain.

I said, "The graduation and the decision that was made is really irrelevant. And it isn't about being perfect. It's about having a system in an organization in which people can legitimately bring up their concerns. And if nothing else, not everybody is always going to give you what you want when you do that, but you will feel heard. But there's no way you can feel heard if all you're doing is talking to each other and not to anybody who can do anything about it. And that's the thing that's disappointing."

Another supervisor spoke up, "If you guys can't take a look at yourself, can't do the work that you need to do on yourself, how can you work with kids? You were sitting up there, you were talking to kids. You were telling kids to confront each other. You were telling kids not to harbor secrets. You were telling kids to get honest, and half you guys can't do that. And I agree that the fishing trip is just the surface. And I think that there's other issues, and that you need to get to Glenna and clean things up."

Judy next directed the restorative questions to one of the staff members who works in the same program, but who did not go on the fishing trip.

"I've done my share of bitching. I've also gotten to Glenna about some of the things. I've also encouraged other people to get to Glenna. So, I don't know where I stand because I know all you guys, and I really like you all as people. But I hated working with all the negativity that's going around."

One of the wrongdoers said, "People look at this as being petty things and, you know, why should I even bring this up, because it's so petty? At least that's the way I look at some things. Like, why should I say to Glenna that it's frustrating when your phone is constantly going off in the middle of a supervision session. That's so petty. You need to get past that. She's got a lot on her plate. Why put one more thing in front of her? But then, I guess that's just one thing that … You start with that, and then it ends up building up with other things."

Then Judy turned to a new staff member. "Matt, you haven't been here that long and I'd like to give you an option to speak. Could you tell us what you've thought about since you heard about this and how you're feeling?"

"This is the first time I'm hearing about it. I remember Monday, the first day, one of the first things Glenna told me was that we work as a team. If you have any problems or any issues, you address them out loud and you tell everyone how you feel. Am I shocked by this? Yeah, for being my third day and seeing everything go on like this. As I'm sitting here, I'm thinking to myself that I could have very well been any one of these people, venting the same way that they vented. I'm glad that I got this opportunity to realize that's not really the way that this place works. And to know this before something like this could ever happen to me. Now I'm back on the other side. I'm really thankful that I am here, and that I got the opportunity to work in what seems to be a very, very good place to work."

Some of the staff who had been complaining about Glenna on the fishing trip, after hearing how their behavior had adversely affected Glenna and others, spoke up again and took greater responsibility. "Glenna, you are not the topic, you are not the focus. You are the person that everyone vented on, and I apologize for that. But you're not the cause of the problems here. And I've been a coward by not speaking my mind about a lot of things. And it's ultimately affecting you, which is totally unfair. And I apologize for that."

Another spoke up. "Another issue we talked about briefly yesterday was mileage. I'm on the road a lot. My car takes a hell of a beating. Gas prices going up, I'm going to be pissed off. I saw gas prices going up and us not being compensated for it. Did I talk to Glenna about it? No. I do take ownership for hearing things and not telling those people to get to whoever they needed to get to about that and handling it inappropriately."

Still another said, "Coming into here, I did have a different way of thinking. The Code of Silence — whatever's said is said for my ears only. And I thought that was a good quality of mine that people can come to me and tell me things and they're not going to get back to that person they were talking about. But obviously, it's a whole different philosophy here."

"I'm going to use this as a learning experience and grow. I think that eventually we will pull together. It probably will take some time to rebuild trust. And I don't know. Just go from there."

"Glenna, what would you like from today's conference?"

"What I need people to do for me to help me grow and help me do my job effectively, I need people to come to me and tell me what their issue or problem is, and we can resolve it. That's what I need."

I had a chance to speak again. "You've heard the expression, 'the squeaky wheel gets the oil.' And that's a good thing. People who squeak a bit get things moving. So please ... would you make a commitment to bring up general concerns to anybody that you think might be able to do something about it? Because it will keep the organization healthy."

Craig, another young supervisor, said, "Some of the people are here that were in the group when the same thing happened to me. Out of crisis came change. People really took this to heart, what happened at the meeting. And it really helped me to grow as a coordinator. And I think the team just really grew. And this continued through team-building, through our meetings that happened every week, and we just kept it going.

"But we each took responsibility for it. And I would just ask that everyone here take responsibility for that. It's not just one person's job. And that it can change, and it can become a lot better. And this horrible feeling that's inside of everyone right now does go away if everybody starts working together."

Another supervisor added, "I guess what I'd like to see is — I challenge everybody individually to take a look at themselves. And to grow and become a better person ... that's something that you ask your kids to do."

Another staff member spoke up. "I just feel like I want to say that I'm sorry to Glenna for just allowing people to talk in my presence. And even joining in at times. And not following up or encouraging them to get to you. Just letting it drop. And just trying to play the middle ground. And I just want to say I'm sorry."

After everyone had an opportunity to speak and personal commitments had been made to improve communication in the future, Judy brought the conference to a conclusion. "I want to thank everybody for all their contributions. I know that this was really difficult for a lot of people. I congratulate you on your participation and what you provided because it is a really important step.

"There are some refreshments over on the table. You can help yourself to those while I write up the agreement. And I'll get to you and have you sign it."

"Thanks, Judy."

"You're welcome."

When the conference ended, everyone breathed a collective sigh of relief. Some people hugged Glenna and others began chatting with one another while they had refreshments.

The time for refreshments is a critical part of a formal restorative event. It provides an opportunity for reintegration after the tension of the conference itself. People smile and laugh and make the transition from formality back to normality.

One Year Later

A year later I conducted a number of videotaped interviews with the conference participants. In carrying out the interviews I made a mistake and did an interview with a woman who was one of the three people who had asked to be edited out of the video that I was producing. When our video editor pointed out my mistake to me I rushed to apologize to the woman. She laughed and said that as time passed she realized that she didn't mind being part of the video. I was pleased because she had said some useful things, both in the conference and in her interview. In fact, the "year later" interviews all were very interesting.

The new counselor who had just started his job days before the conference said, "At first, I felt like, oh man, there's something that they did wrong, and they're going to get fired for it. Or they're going to get in trouble for it. And they're never going to live that moment down. But as the conference went on, I grew to understand that there's a purpose to this. There's a strong meaning to this. It's going to be dealt with today, and we're going to learn from this experience."

Rich, who had been the first to speak in the conference, remembered, "I don't think they were owning up to much, myself included. The supporters of Glenna and other employees had their say, and they had some powerful statements that impacted the people who were being confronted. So I think the mood changed. It went from being stale and not much sincerity or not much concern, to where it started progressing, where finally I took a look at myself."

Another staff member observed, "About the people that took responsibility, it felt almost like a cleansing. It was refreshing. It was like, OK, let's get rid of the negativity."

Others concurred, "I took responsibility for it. Let's move on. I learned more about myself. And I saw the pain that Glenna had gone through. Knowing not only did it affect her, it affected everyone that was on her side as support. You don't realize that things like this can affect more than just one person."

"As the conference was going on, hearing the genuineness of the people in the room, I started thinking, 'This is a good thing. This is a good conclusion of it.' I felt great. It was very good."

"It was almost like a big weight was lifted towards the end of the conference. The mood went from being very tense to being more relaxed. It was almost like, 'Wow, I'm really glad that happened.'"

"It was the anniversary of the conference not too long ago and you can see the changes from a year ago to now. As far as people getting to supervisors with different issues and things of that sort, I've watched some counselors really take charge and make changes. And I've watched other counselors decide — make choices for themselves that they didn't want to stay with the agency because they didn't want to follow the norms of the agency or didn't believe in the norms of the agency. And that's really OK, too."

Glenna herself said, "I think the valuable impact coming out of the conference was that relationships improved. There was trust-building. The staff that I've worked with, they can confront one another now and don't feel threatened."

Another staff member commented, "If we'd never had that conference, I don't think people would be aware of the dangers of talking behind people's back or handling the situation in the wrong way. I know I wouldn't be aware of it. And being my third day at work, I'm like, 'Wow, this is a neat experience. This is a neat workplace. This is an awesome place to work.'"

"The long-term effects, I think, are it brings closure to certain issues. It allows people to get rid of resentments they might hold. It just allows for a better working environment and more personal interaction. Like, getting to know people more. It's just a more healthy environment [in which] to work."

Restorative Leadership and Fair Process

The fishing trip incident and the restorative conference that dealt with it also had significant implications for those of us who lead the IIRP consortium of organizations, including Community Service Foundation (CSF) and Buxmont Academy, which operate our programs for delinquent and at-risk youth. Because there had been a similar incident only five years before in the CSF Supervision Program, we reflected about what we were doing wrong.

We recognized that it was our responsibility to ensure that new staff learn the values of the organization, give them practice and opportunities to bring up their concerns in a timely, appropriate manner and prevent conflicts that disrupt the workplace. What is unique about the Supervision Program's employees, relative to other CSF Buxmont employees, is that they travel a great deal, visiting their clients in many different locales. They do not spend as much time working together in one location as staff in our other programs. So we realized that we were going to have to work extra hard at orientation and teambuilding in the Supervision Program. In the decade since the conference, the morale and spirit of cooperation in that program has been good and there has not been another incident of this nature.

Because most of us spend a large part of our lives in our workplaces, we want them to be pleasant. Unfortunately workplaces are often rife with conflict, both overt and secretive. Restorative practices have the potential to help leaders manage and resolve those conflicts and foster a sense of fairness and trust, not only for our own sake as individuals, but for the sake of the organization as well — to make it more productive.

Restorative practices embody the three steps of "fair process" — engagement, explanation and expectation clarity — cited earlier in this book from the *Harvard Business Review* article of that title. Significantly, the article is subtitled "Managing in the Knowledge Economy." As agencies that work with learning and behavior change, the IIRP and its sister agencies, Community Service Foundation and Buxmont Academy, have tried to live by restorative values because, according to the article, doing so creates the positive atmosphere that "influences attitudes and behaviors that are critical to high performance."[71]

The article asserts that without a strong sense of fairness and trust in a workplace, employees are less likely to cooperate, share their creativity and take risks in making suggestions for improvement: "It is easy to see fair process at work on the plant floor, where its violation can produce such highly visible manifestations as strikes, slowdowns, and high defect rates. But fair process can have an even greater impact on the quality of professional and managerial work."[72]

The attitude toward administration inherent in restorative practices and fair process clashes with traditional management strategies that assume people are basically lazy and untrustworthy. Those strategies rely on rigid hierarchy, strict enforcement of authoritarian rules and a system of punishments and rewards.[73] While fully recognizing the importance of authority, we also know that simply telling people to "do what I say because I say so" is not effective leadership. We achieve much better results when we exercise our authority with grace — allowing people to appropriately voice their concerns, giving them an explanation for a decision and being clear about what we expect from them.

"Expectation clarity" is a critical issue. At our CSF Buxmont programs, for example, on the first day an employee reports to work in one of our programs for delinquent and at-risk youth, a supervisor reviews a written document entitled "Basic Concepts." That document defines specific behaviors that will maximize that staff person's effectiveness with our clients. Our teenage clients are often manipulative and divisive with adults, particularly when they are newly enrolled. Here is the text of our Basic Concepts:

> The ideas presented below are fundamental to our agency philosophy and processes:
> - We believe that people are capable of growing and learning in their work and behavior.
> - We, as staff members, trust each other. We maintain a healthy skepticism when clients criticize other staff members. Our first assumption should be that we are not hearing an accurate version of events from the adolescent, which is usually how it works out. If we have any concerns about another staff member, we do not share them with the client. We check out our concerns privately with that staff member.
> - If we do have a legitimate concern about a fellow staff member's behavior, we should present the concern to them directly or seek supervision.
> - We do not keep secrets or collude with clients. We must share information with every one else in the organization who is working with them. (An exception: When a client tells us they are HIV positive, we only discuss it with our supervisor and with others on a need-to-know basis.)

> We act as role models by participating in activities with our clients. This includes taking risks, sharing feelings and having fun.

> We respond to situations WITH our clients, not TO them or FOR them.

> We avoid power struggles with clients.

> We separate the deed from the doer by affirming the worth of the individual while disapproving of the inappropriate behavior.

> We avoid the roles in the "blame game." We avoid being "rescuers" and do not perceive others as "persecutors," because that allows our clients to see themselves as "victims." Rather, we encourage our clients to experience the consequences when they make poor choices. We encourage our clients to see themselves as having the power to make positive choices and take control of their own lives.

> Whenever we hear dangerous or life-threatening information, we involve our supervisors and others in the decision-making process and as quickly as possible share the information with all the other professionals dealing with the relevant clients.

> We are not expected to have all the answers. Instead of trying to answer or act without adequate knowledge, we need to ask others for help.

> We understand that we will occasionally disagree with our referral sources, such as probation officers or caseworkers, and we should seek supervision in resolving the issue.

> We avoid alienating parents. Whenever possible we try to align ourselves with them. We patiently advise them of the situation. We help them understand our organization's philosophy and processes.

> Human beings function best in an environment that encourages free expression of emotion — minimizing

the negative, maximizing the positive, but allowing people to say what is really on their minds.

The reasons underlying the Basic Concepts are beyond the scope of this book. I present them here to illustrate the need to be explicit about expectations. More than a decade ago, our CSF Buxmont staff went through a participatory process to write these Basic Concepts, especially for the benefit of our new employees. The final document was deliberately limited to one page because multipage documents and manuals do not capture people's attention as easily. While a detailed manual also can be useful, it serves a different purpose. We identified critical behaviors that could fit on one sheet of paper, so that new staff would readily notice and remember them. Then, as issues arose, they would be able to relate those situations to what they had read. In training for new staff, there may be a circle in which each person is asked to choose a basic concept and talk about it, as a way of ensuring that everyone fully understands the expectations.

The same "expectation clarity" is embodied in the "Basic Concepts for Supervision" document for organizational leaders, developed in another participatory process by those of us in leadership roles in the IIRP's consortium of organizations:

The ideas presented below are fundamental to supervising staff in our agency:

> Staff members are capable of growing and changing.
> People benefit from, and actually welcome, honest feedback.
> Feedback should be given to staff members as soon as possible and be as concrete as possible.
> We help employees develop competencies rather than providing the answers for them.
> We hold employees accountable for their behavior in a restorative manner.
> We readily ask our supervisor for help in supervising staff.

> We act as role models for our staff by admitting when we are wrong and being humble.
> Staff members will sometimes be unhappy with the decisions we as supervisors make.
> We understand the boundaries between management and staff and take seriously our responsibility to the organization.
> We are willing to address any issue with our staff even if they are likely to be embarrassing or difficult to hear.
> People's personal issues will come up at work. Most issues we need to address have come up for the employee sometime before in their life.
> Supervisors help people face change rather than insulating them from change.
> Part of our job is to make more leaders in the organization.
> We readily share concerns about employees with the appropriate supervisor(s).
> Supervisors are willing to confront each other.

Restorative Responses to Mistakes and Wrongdoing

In stark contrast to a system of punishment and rewards, we engage with our employees when dealing with mistakes or wrongdoing. Just as we deal with students in a restorative disciplinary system, we do not scold in our workplace. Rather, we ask open-ended questions and let the wrongdoer speak. We treat mistakes as part of a learning process and help people determine what they should do differently in the future.

"What happened?" and "What were you thinking about at the time?" provide a useful and respectful way to address mistakes or lapses in judgment. Asking other questions to explore "Who has been affected?" and "How have they been affected?" provides people with empathy and insight into the consequences of their actions. And lastly, getting them to talk about how to resolve the issue or clean up the bad feelings they may have caused, allows them the opportunity to redeem themselves.

It would take another book to thoroughly explore all the variations of wrongdoing and the ways that people respond. In a workplace that already has a high level of trust, most people respond honestly and with the best of intentions. Others distort the truth or outright lie or try to avoid responsibility. Occasionally an offense is so substantial that the police or other authorities must become involved. Sometimes a person must be fired. But without exception, treating people with respect works best.

Out of each crisis arises both danger and opportunity. We are mindful that all of our staff watch how our leaders address a problem. Handling problems without using fair process has negative consequences. However, if leaders treat staff mistakes and wrongdoing with fairness and show respect for people's dignity, they will both resolve the threat to the well-being of the organization and simultaneously build trust and loyalty among all the staff.

Letter of Understanding

One of our staff had worked with us for more than a decade when, in a change of organizational structure, a newly hired supervisor became her boss. The manager struggled with the change. She was jealous that her new supervisor was now handling matters that used to be hers alone to decide. At times she tried to undermine her boss, compete with her, criticize her ideas or distract from her agenda at meetings. Her supervisor challenged the inappropriate behavior in private discussions that seemed to go well — but sometimes the angry outbursts reoccurred. The supervisor decided to ask the employee to address the issues by writing a "letter of understanding."

The three primary elements featured in our organization's letter of understanding mirror the restorative questions. The employee is asked to identify the inappropriate behavior, recognize who has been affected and how, and make a plan for resolving the problem. When mistakes or misdeeds are substantial or recurring, making the

restorative process written, instead of verbal, emphasizes the serious-
ness of the situation.

The letter of understanding shifts responsibility from the supervisor to the employee. Most people accept that responsibility gra-
ciously and realize that they are being given an opportunity to fix
the problem rather put their job in jeopardy. For a few, being honest
and explicit is difficult. They attempt to gloss over unpleasant facts
and make excuses. The supervisor reviews the letter after the first
draft and points out what needs improvement — sometimes asking
for multiple revisions. At some point reluctant writers recognize that
they will need to get honest, with themselves and their boss, and
move forward.

The letter of understanding makes abstract matters tangible. In
the future, the supervisor can sit down with the employee and the
letter to review his or her progress with clarity. Time does not dimin-
ish or change the understanding, as can readily happen in verbal
exchanges, nor are the issues in dispute, because every word in the
document belongs to its author. Even if some parts of the letter are
written at the insistence of the supervisor, in the end the employee
signs the letter and agrees to its provisions.

In our "Guidelines for Preparing a Letter of Understanding" we
explain to our supervisors: "When a mistake, conflict or incident of
wrongdoing occurs in the workplace, a letter of understanding can
transform that incident into a significant opportunity for learning."
What is unique about our approach is that while the employee gets a
copy of the letter, we keep our copy sealed in an envelope in a confi-
dential part of their personnel file. Although we maintain personnel
files for ten years after a person leaves employment, we immediately
destroy any letters of understanding. The letter of understanding is
not a punishment nor does it leave a negative mark in the employee's
record. Sometimes our employees volunteer to write a letter of understanding when they find themselves struggling with a work issue that
they themselves have identified. They have come to see the letter of
understanding as a vehicle for personal growth.

In this instance, the employee's first draft of the letter of understanding to her supervisor was excellent. She wrote about herself with great self-awareness and brutal candor, describing her problem behavior, her underlying feelings, her impact on others and her commitment to change.

"I lost my temper, I lost control and I said terribly hurtful things which were absolutely uncalled for and which I certainly should not have said. This was in reaction to feelings of shame. ... This is something I've been dealing with for months — the feeling of shame on being left out. I feel childish and stupid and worthless every time for even having that feeling.

"I now realize I also wanted attention, which I got: the worst kind. I made everyone feel bad about themselves — and about me. I have felt horrible ever since: sick, worthless, disgusting and sad. I want to say to you now that I am very, very sorry for what I did.

"I understand that you have been feeling undermined by me for some time, including in the last Monday morning meeting. I admit I was not aware of this. Reflecting on it, however, I can see that I probably have been doing it in an attempt to make myself feel more important (but actually having exactly the opposite effect).

"I make a commitment to trusting you. ... I want you to know that I think you're doing an amazing job leading our group, and that we really need what you bring to it and to the organization as a whole. You're a great leader. There: I said it, and I mean it. I'm glad you're here, because you're really helping us move forward. I actually really like working with you! You set clear expectations, which I really appreciate. ... I hereby make a commitment to support you in leading our group and to leave my attitude issues behind. I think that's the best thing I can do to help the organization move forward, as well as for myself and for my relationship with you and with others in the organization."

As is almost always the case, the letter of understanding helped a valued employee identify and resolve issues that were troubling both her and the organization. She has grown beyond the problem and the related inappropriate behaviors.

Restorative Feedback and Evaluation

Creating an atmosphere in which employees and their supervisors view mistakes as opportunities for personal growth is not easy to attain. Restorative feedback and evaluation are essential facets of such a workplace. A popular management book, *The One Minute Manager,* describes feedback as "the breakfast of champions." Good leaders provide feedback that is timely and truthful.[74] We concur. A supervisor's external critique and praise are critical to helping people improve. But there are also times when we give employees opportunities to reflect and express the issues themselves. People can be remarkably self-aware and articulate about their own shortcomings and how they might improve themselves.

Our annual evaluation process embraces that perspective. Staff take the first step by writing their own self-evaluation. They respond to a set of standard questions appropriate to their particular employee group with a "reflection" and a "goal" for each. Supervisors read the evaluations and respond with written comments that affirm, challenge or add suggestions. There are no financial implications associated with this annual evaluation — it's just about personal growth.

In our graduate school, for example, a faculty member reflects and set goals in response to questions such as:

> Am I restorative in my relationships with students, faculty, administrators and board members?
> How do I model the ideals of restorative practices?
> Do I provide appropriate assistance to students? Do I make myself readily available?
> How have I advanced the academic fields in which I am involved?
> Do I adequately prepare for my courses? Is my course material creative, current and interesting?
> What am I doing to advance my professional growth?

In all of our organizations, an administrator responds to equivalent questions such as:

> Am I restorative in my relationships with students, faculty, administrators and board members?
> How do I model the ideals of restorative practices?
> Do I provide appropriate assistance to students, faculty, staff and other administrators? Do I make myself readily available?
> Do I appropriately carry out my administrative responsibilities?
> Do I demonstrate initiative in my work?
> What am I doing to advance my professional growth?

Clerical and support staff reflect and set goals in response to:
> *Initiative* (Are you open to new ideas or try new approaches? Do you ask for help and suggestions? Do you offer ideas and suggestions? Are you flexible?)
> *Communication* (Do you readily give and receive feedback? — both criticism and praise? How are your written skills? How are your verbal skills? How is your rapport with students, co-workers and others? Do you greet people when they come in? Can you give criticism and praise? How are you on the phone?)
> *Dependability/Work Performance* (Do you have good attendance? Are you on time with tasks? Can you be counted on to follow through on work assignments? Do you tend to details? Are you organized? Can you prioritize your work assignments? Do you know the limits of your responsibilities? Are you able to use general knowledge to handle unplanned situations? Are you able to gain knowledge from past experience and apply them to future situations?)

Self-evaluation fosters self-responsibility. A thoughtful self-evaluation should elicit mostly affirmations from a boss. If a supervisor has been doing his or her job all year and bringing up concerns in a timely fashion, employees know exactly what is expected of them and in which areas they need to improve. There should be no surprises. In the self-evaluation employees may demonstrate, in their own voices, that they have reflected on their strengths and weaknesses and have set goals accordingly.

Circles in the Workplace

When an individual's behavior adversely affects others in the workplace, usually one-to-one feedback is sufficient. On rare occasions a formal restorative process like the workplace conference is necessary. The fishing trip incident caused such a stir in our organization and angered so many people that we opted for a conference, but we have only convened a couple of formal conferences in the decade since then.

Restorative circles are less formal and require less preparation than a conference, but they provide an effective way to deal with problems that require more than individual feedback. They are also the appropriate choice when we are not clear about who is in the wrong. Just like circles in schools, workplace circles provide everyone with a setting where they express feelings and gain an understanding of how others feel. Because people can only speak when it is their turn and the order of speakers is dictated by simply going around the circle, the process provides decorum and safety. A "talking piece" handed around the circle clearly designates who has the right to speak, improving the likelihood that people will honor the process. People do not argue and yell. They listen and wait their turn to speak.

A circle about a staff member's frequent absences, for example, allowed that person to understand how others were affected by her frequent days off and how disruptive it was to the workplace. She improved her attendance — not because her boss threatened her but as a result of both peer pressure and the realization that her absences impacted others in her workplace.

Skeptics understandably question the circle's effectiveness, finding it hard to believe that such a simple process could be so reliable. Few have experienced a setting where they may speak without interruption and must listen without immediately responding. Only when we actually participate in this unique community forum can we fully appreciate its power.

Circles have many other applications in the workplace. Quality circles, originally associated with Japanese manufacturing, are one of the most well-known "restorative" innovations in the corporate world. Quality circles encourage production workers to participate in company matters so that management can benefit from production workers' intimate knowledge of the production process.[75] While credited with boosting the fortunes of Japanese companies in the decades following World War II, quality circles became a passing fad among U.S. corporations that failed because the circles had no real power or voice, according to Harvey Robbins and Michael Finley, in *Why The New Teams Don't Work*. They assert that "In the best teams you see a circle. ... When people take the time to learn about one another, what is in their hearts as well as in their minds, we rise to a higher level."[76]

Circles are useful in teambuilding — proactively building social capital. Social capital is the connection among individuals and the trust, mutual understanding, shared values and behaviors that bind us together and make cooperative action possible.[77] At CSF Buxmont and the IIRP we usually hold monthly teambuilding circles at each worksite in which individuals take responsibility for running an hour-long exercise or game that allows people to get to know one another better.

At the beginning of regular meetings we do a "check-in," usually a couple of minutes long, in which each person reports briefly how he or she is feeling that morning or mentions something notable in their work or personal lives. It helps people shift their attention from their private thoughts to the process of the group. At the close of the meeting a brief "check-out" process summarizes group members' perceptions about the meeting they just attended.

Even in the midst of meetings, after a tumultuous discussion in which ideas gush forth and even clash, we sometimes pause and do a circle process to ascertain the group's mind-set — each person speaking without interruption and with everyone listening carefully to what is said. The decorum created by the circle process allows individuals to transition from the spirited discussion to a thoughtful recap. The overall effect centers everyone and summarizes the content, so subsequent discussion proceeds from a new level of mutual understanding.

A couple of years ago I served as consultant to the governing board of a new alternative school. They wanted to use restorative practices in their meetings so they could begin to understand the strategies the staff would be using with the students. We arranged the meeting room with a circle of chairs, did an introductory go-around, but otherwise conducted the meeting with conventional procedures. After a heated discussion involving several contentious issues, I asked everyone to go around the circle, each expressing their current thoughts. A calm settled over the room. A couple of individuals who had been particularly challenging toward others, without prompting, apologized for their cantankerous behavior. Their apologies were acknowledged by smiles and nodding heads. By the time the circle was completed there was a clear consensus on key issues that had not been apparent earlier. Unanimous votes led quickly toward adjournment.

Ending Employment Restoratively

Unfortunately, there are lots of examples of how not to end people's employment. Here is a story from the *New Yorker* magazine:

On October 2nd workers at the Ashland plant went home after a normal day. When they arrived for the morning shift on October 3rd, they found the gates locked and a message on the factory's information number saying that the factory was closed. The following day, all two hundred and seventy-eight employees received a certified letter terminating their employment, effective immediately.[78]

In our own organization we have tried to behave differently, consistent with our restorative philosophy. We have often engaged staff when dealing with financial challenges. For example, one department was faced with a cut-off in funds by a juvenile probation department near the end of the fiscal year. The abrupt revenue shortfall would have required several staff layoffs for a couple of months. All of the full-time employees, most of whom also did additional part-time work for our organization as a way of supplementing their salaries, decided to share that work with those threatened with layoffs. In that way, everyone kept full-time employment for the remainder of the fiscal year. Rather than the leadership imposing a solution, our employees creatively solved the problem themselves.

After the 2008 banking crisis we shared details of our challenging financial situation with employees at CSF Buxmont and the IIRP. We assured people that we would keep them informed but encouraged those with the most vulnerable jobs to look for employment. In exchange for openness about our financial situation, we asked that people keep us advised of their intentions, so we were not surprised by sudden departures. The risk of our candor was that essential people would leave for a more secure job.

For a while, the number of people leaving voluntarily largely matched our declining revenue, but in the fall of 2011 CSF Buxmont's school and residential programs opened the school year with a dramatic downturn in enrollment. This situation was so dire that it was not realistic to involve the staff in seeking a creative short-term solution. Layoffs were inevitable. A few weeks later we announced, through the managers at each of our worksites, the names of the employees who would be laid off. We simultaneously invited everyone in the organization to a meeting the next day in a central location.

The three primary leaders of CSF Buxmont and the IIRP, Judy Happ, Craig Adamson and I, spoke to the group of more than a hundred people who chose to come to the meeting. We made some preliminary remarks and then explained that we would now take their questions and comments. We would write everything on large flip-chart sheets and withhold comment until everyone was done. We urged them to be as candid and challenging as they needed to be.

When everyone was finished commenting, we responded. One woman said that she thought she should have received a personal phone call from one of us, rather than hearing the news through her manager. Without getting defensive, we acknowledged her feelings and explained why we did what we did. Another person asked why we had spent money to renovate two classrooms in a building recently. Again, trying to avoid defensiveness, we provided the rationale. Still others wanted to know more details about the current financial situation and whether there would be further layoffs. We said that there likely would be at least a few more people laid off in the coming weeks, unless there was a dramatic improvement in revenue. We explained that people could ask their manager to give them an honest assessment of how vulnerable they were. Someone asked about our criteria for deciding who got laid off. We explained that people with the least seniority were the most vulnerable, but there were other factors such as specialized skills, teaching certificates or other credentials essential to our continued operations. One young man who had not lost his job asked a remarkably candid question: Did we, the three leaders, think we were the right people, with the right experience and skills to see us through these difficult financial times? I answered for the three of us. I acknowledged that his was the key question, that I thought we were the right people, that I really didn't know who else to turn to who knew more about our businesses than we did — but that only time would tell if we were making good decisions.

Most of the comments were positive in tone, acknowledging that what was happening to us was happening everywhere, that they appreciated the honest and open way we were dealing with the crisis. In contrast, they said they had friends or family members who had been abruptly laid off without even a hint that their jobs were in jeopardy. Also, although our organization had no obligation to do so, we announced that everyone who was leaving would receive severance pay.

We had placed large envelopes with the name of each person who was being laid off on tables in the back of the room. As the meeting closed, we provided paper and pens and offered people the opportunity to write messages and put them in individual envelopes. The next day, each worksite organized good-bye circles in which all of the individuals who were leaving had a chance to hear good-byes and comments from their co-workers and to respond. These rituals provide people with a chance to communicate with one another and have a sense of closure, instead of an unceremonious departure.

After more than three decades of growth, the darkening shadows of recession forced us to lay off people for the first time in our organizations' history. As my Australian friend Terry O'Connell once noted, "There's really no nice way to poke someone in the eye." Being laid off is surely a poke in the eye. But we held the meeting and provided rituals to ensure, even though people were leaving their jobs involuntarily, that they felt they had worked for a good company that valued them, respected their dignity and provided engagement, explanation and expectation clarity.

Evidence

The "Fair Process" article in *Harvard Business Review* was based on a study of strategic decision making in 19 multinational companies. The research concluded, "Managers who believed the company's processes were fair displayed a high level of trust and commitment, which in turn engendered active cooperation. Conversely, when managers felt fair process was absent, they hoarded ideas and dragged their feet."[79] In subsequent field research, the authors identified the three principles of fair process and affirmed their findings.

Two contrasting case studies from their research illustrate the significance of restorative practices values in organizations. In the summer of 1992, at Volkswagen's Puebla, Mexico, manufacturing facility, workers turned against both their union and the company, despite a generous 20 percent wage increase offer. The "union's leaders had not involved employees in discussions about the contract's terms," especially a number of unexplained work-rule changes that the workers feared. A massive walkout cost the company about 10 million dollars per day and disrupted its optimistic plans for the U.S. market.[80]

Troubled Siemens Nixdorf Informationssysteme, on the other hand, had cut 17,000 jobs by 1994, when Gerhard Schulmeyer, the new CEO, held a series of meetings, large and small, in which he personally explained to 11,000 of the company's remaining 32,000 employees the bleak outlook and the need to make deep cuts. He asked for volunteers to come up with ideas to save the company. The initial group of 30 volunteers grew to 9,000 employees and managers who met mostly after business hours, often until midnight. They offered their ideas to executives who could choose to finance them or not. Although 20 to 30 percent of their ideas were rejected, the executives explained the reasons for their decisions, so people felt the process was fair. By the next year the company was operating in the black again and employee satisfaction had doubled, despite the drastic changes underway — "a transformation notable in European corporate history."[81]

Another research project in the *Harvard Business Review* reported that "Leadership is a conversation." Based on interviews over two years with 150 top leaders at 100 companies, the researchers concluded: "Smart leaders today, we have found, engage with employees in a way that resembles an ordinary person-to-person conversation more than it does a series of commands from on high. Furthermore they initiate practices and foster cultural norms that instill a conversational sensibility throughout their organizations."

The authors define four key elements of organizational conversation: *intimacy, interactivity, inclusion and intentionality.*[82] The four elements, along with the author's examples, are congruent with restorative practices.

Intimacy requires "getting close" and "gaining trust." Medical-records technology provider Atheneahealth shares strategic and financial information, usually provided to only top leaders in most companies, so that their employees are thoroughly involved in the business. Duke Energy's president and CEO, James E. Rogers, manifested other aspects of intimacy, "listening well" and "getting personal," by instituting a series of three-hour listening sessions in which he invited participants to raise pressing issues. He also asked employees for feedback on his own performance.

Interactivity involves "promoting dialogue." In some companies leaders have fostered a genuinely interactive culture — values, norms and behaviors that welcome dialogue. Because it is more challenging to promote interaction within large companies, Cisco Systems uses a specialized video technology for remote interpersonal exchange, which ensures that the on-screen images of people appear life-size and thereby more personal and realistic.

Inclusion expands employees' roles as "executives cede a fair amount of control over how the company is represented to the world." Employees are encouraged to act as company ambassadors, to be thought leaders and to tell their own stories. Scott Huennekens, the CEO of Volcano Corporation, a medical technology company, says that such an approach "has made organizational life less stifling and more productive than it used to be."

With regard to *intentionality*, "The conversation that unfolds within a company should reflect a shared agenda that aligns with the company's strategic objectives." To that end, for example, Infosys includes a broad range of employees, from every rank and division, in the company's annual strategy-development process.[83]

In a university study that set out to find the best workplaces in Australia and then analyze their basis for excellence, the researchers concluded: "After assessing the results of our field research and interviews we concluded that quality working relationships represent the central pivot on which excellent workplaces are founded, underpinned by key variables such as good workplace leadership, clear values, having a say and being safe."[84] They clarify that "it is very important to understand that when talking about relationships at work we are not talking about friendships alone. ... The fundamental relationships built on that magic word — trust — couldn't be overestimated."[85]

While these researchers would not have been familiar with the term "restorative practices," the values and practices they surveyed in businesses perfectly match the values and practices we have been developing over the last three decades at CSF Buxmont and the IIRP. Their findings fully concur with our fundamental premise — the best outcomes are achieved when those in authority do things *with* people, not *to* them or *for* them.

Building Campus Community

Chapter 7
Building Campus Community[86]

Campus Conference

In the first year that restorative practices were implemented at the University of Vermont (UVM), a student who was skateboarding in a hallway, in violation of residential rules, inadvertently hit a sprinkler head. Water surged through the hallway into bedrooms. Firefighters arrived and the building was evacuated. Students could not return to their rooms until 4 a.m., with ten rooms suffering such serious water damage that those residents had to sleep in other quarters. Books, clothing, laptop computers and beds were damaged or destroyed.

Although the student came forward to admit what he had done and his family's homeowners insurance reimbursed the losses, the young man was ashamed to face his peers. Students were angry and upset, as rumors further exacerbated feelings by creating distorted accounts of what had actually happened. While the authorities did not plan to impose punitive sanctions, in the past such an incident would result in the young man moving to another residence hall in an effort to avoid the stigma. But since the advent of restorative practices at UVM, the residential life staff now had a more effective way to deal with the emotional aftermath, by inviting the young man to participate in a restorative conference.

The conference was scheduled for a Sunday evening with 30 participants, including all the students whose rooms and property had been damaged. The young man's roommate and his resident advisor (RA) were both there to support him. The staff that organized and facilitated the conference appropriately prepared everyone beforehand by letting them all know what to expect.

The skateboarder had the first opportunity to speak. When the other students realized that the incident was truly an accident, their anger subsided. Contrary to the rumors, the young man had done nothing deliberate. While he was not supposed to be skateboarding in the hallway, the consequence was obviously unintentional. He had no way of anticipating the extensive damage that his inappropriate actions would cause. As the other students spoke, he had an opportunity to truly understand how he had adversely affected so many people in his residential community.

The conference facilitator reported that the conference went better than she had expected. The next day the student sent her an email saying, "I was skeptical going into the conference. However, I'm really glad that I was able to participate in this and I really understand how my actions affected my neighbors and fellow students." Satisfaction over the resolution of the incident was high because the conference resolved angry feelings, allowed the offender to be reintegrated into his community of peers, and put the whole incident to rest.

The Challenge of Residence Life

Every year during the summer orientation program, Stacey Miller, director of residential life at UVM, tells parents of new students the unvarnished truth — that even under the best of circumstances, living in a campus residence hall is a difficult undertaking. Many parents, some being former college students, nod in agreement. She goes on to describe the residence hall as a unique environment where almost everyone is in young adulthood — no children, middle-aged adults, elders and, except for aquarium fish, no pets. Yet new students enthusiastically embrace this artificial reality because their goal is simple: They want to escape parents, family members and any kind of adult authority in their quest for independence and adulthood.

Those of us who have already experienced college life are painfully aware that, without the right support systems, residence hall living can be a recipe for disaster. Why? Because people who are in youthful stages of their emotional, mental and social development often behave in ways that are not socially responsible, civil or respectful — of themselves or others. To envision how easily civilization can turn to chaos when the young are left to their own devices, one only has to remember the boys who devolved into savagery in William Golding's classic novel *Lord of the Flies*.

Every year college and university residence halls open their doors to hundreds of thousands of first-year students who will occupy shared living settings with a population density more concentrated than most urban apartment buildings. With the exception of a few encounters at orientation or through Facebook exchanges, most of these students do not know each other. Nor have most of them ever lived away from their families, except for a summer camp experience. More and more students entering college have never shared a bedroom with a sibling and in some instances have never even shared a bathroom. Outside of directed social group activities or participation on a sports team, most have not had to live or work cooperatively with members of their peer group.

Some students have problems with alcohol and drug use. Others are boisterous, noisy, messy and rude. Some struggle with personal relationships or mental health issues or hold racial and religious biases that interfere with their ability to connect with others. Others come with even more serious problems, a history of stealing or violence that is not disclosed, which eventually manifests itself in the close quarters of residential living. In some ways residential hall living and the students who occupy these spaces are just a microcosm of the larger world, but with the inherent behaviors and characteristics of youth. Soon after their arrival on campus, students will face the demands and stresses of their academic programs — classes, assignments, exams and papers — and tensions and conflicts with roommates and friends. These are the circumstances that, every year, frame the fundamental challenge faced by the residential life staff at colleges and universities: how to build healthy communities quickly and effectively so that students can live together productively and harmoniously.

Community Standards

As a student affairs practitioner for more than 17 years, Stacey Miller spent much of her career in residential life looking for a formula that would enable students in residential settings, at a minimum, to get along with each other. Many years ago she found half of that formula for healthy residential communities in the theoretical model known as "community standards." Developed at the University of Nevada, the community standards process allows students to create mutually agreed-upon expectations that define how their "community will engage and function on an interpersonal level." The model relies on dialogue to create and maintain standards because peer-to-peer interaction has been found to be the "single most potent source of influence on growth and development during the undergraduate years,"[87] and the simple act of sharing feelings can influence and change peer perspectives and behaviors.

Through the community standards process, community members meet to discuss their needs and wants as they relate to residence hall living, make agreements based on these needs and wants, and resolve difficulties that arise when agreements are not honored. Use of the community standards model is supposed to change the role of staff from authorities to facilitators and the role of students from recipients to creators of their own experiences. Theoretically, staff members are no longer expected to control, but rather guide the community toward individual and group responsibility and accountability.[88]

But what sounded great in theory was difficult to implement in practice. Residential life professional staff members must train young resident advisors (RAs), who are in the inherently ambiguous and frustrating position of simultaneously being both peer support and authorities in their relationships with the other students in their living area, to implement the community standards process. Often relying on an implicit understanding of how to develop community, residential life professional staff members would often tell RAs to build community, but struggle to explicitly show them how. RAs were then left to figure out their own strategies and techniques to bring students together.

While some RAs are naturally communicative or charismatic, few are prepared to herd 50 or more diverse 18- to 22-year-olds together and run a meeting for any sustained period of time. How do RAs create an environment where boisterous, bored, distracted, impatient, posturing, nervous and occasionally "too cool for school" young adults will engage in meaningful dialogue about issues like roommate relationships, cleanliness and vandalism? Stacey Miller found the answer to that question — the second half of the formula — in restorative practices.

Implementing Restorative Practices at UVM

Stacey Miller first encountered restorative practices when she participated in a 15-minute circle facilitated by the Vermont safe schools consultant, in which she says she learned more about some of her colleagues than she had known in the eight years she had worked with them. The circle was simple, structured and provided equal status for all the participants. While the facilitator took part in the conversation, he did not dominate or artificially control it. Rather, the "talking piece," as it was passed around the circle from person to person, ensured that respect was paid to each individual who was talking while they held the object. Although the circle is but one aspect of the restorative practices framework, it is a very symbolic and powerful mechanism to help students get to know each other and begin the process of openly discussing their needs and wants — consistent with the community standards process.

In collaboration with the IIRP, UVM's residential life staff began using restorative practices both proactively and reactively. Pleased with the first year's results, UVM institutionalized restorative practices so that each August RAs will participate in three days of IIRP-designed restorative practices training. In accordance with the IIRP's commitment to developing local training capacity, UVM staff has taken over the training responsibility. The training and related book given to each RA teaches them how to begin the school year with proactive circles that foster community standards and also how to use a range of informal and formal restorative practices to respond to problems, conflicts and wrongdoing as they arise.

The initial circle of the school year is held with first-year students when they arrive. Passing a talking piece around the circle, RAs ask them to respond to questions like: "What are you hoping for in your first year here?" "What are your concerns?" "What are some of your long-term hopes and dreams?" These simple questions allow students to share as much or as little of themselves as they choose, while providing opportunities for students to become acquainted with each other and with the restorative circles that will be held periodically in their residence halls during the school year.

A few days later, when returning students join first-year students in the residence halls, RAs hold circles with questions designed to establish and support the community standards process: "What do you think the ideal residential community looks like?" "What kind of behaviors might interfere with achieving that ideal community? "What can we as individuals and as a group do to overcome those obstacles to achieving an ideal community?" Those unfamiliar with circles are often surprised by how engaged students quickly become in addressing and solving behavioral issues and conflicts that are usually considered the domain of those in positions of authority.

UVM residential life staff use circles throughout the school year for a variety of purposes: to foster positive relationships, to raise consciousness about bias issues and to respond to conflicts and problems. The key to a successful circle is for facilitators to be clear in their own minds what the goal of each circle is going to be and then structure questions that promote that goal.

In response to substantial incidents of wrongdoing, UVM staff members have decided on two strategies. They use circles when they do not know the identity of the wrongdoer and formal restorative conferences when they do. When there is anonymous vandalism or bias graffiti, RAs convene a circle that allows students to express their feelings about the situation and to brainstorm ideas to prevent a reoccurrence. The culprit is often in the circle, hearing others' responses to their actions and gaining an understanding of how they have adversely affected their peers. That understanding and perhaps the fear of being discovered often discourage further problems.

When the wrongdoer is known, the formal restorative conference has greater impact and is more complete. The conference facilitator asks a series of open-ended restorative questions that provide everyone with an opportunity to express themselves: first the offender, followed by those directly harmed, their supporters and then those who are there to support the offender. Lastly, everyone has an opportunity to discuss what actions might help to repair the harm. After the formal conference refreshments are served, providing an opportunity for informal conversation and social reintegration.

Lesser problems in the residence halls are handled more informally. RAs might respond to loud music or late night commotion or other violations with simple affective statements, telling students how their behavior makes them feel. Or they might be slightly more formal, asking a restorative question derived from the formal conference script, such as "How do you think you are affecting others?" or after exploring feelings, "How can you make things right?" Or they might move to a small impromptu conference, bringing a few people together for an exchange, using the restorative questions to frame the discussion.

For some, being restorative is not a comfortable way of confronting behavior. For decades housing professionals have taught RAs to "lay down the law" and simply stop negative behavior. With a *to* approach, the RA is the "boss," the person who is in charge of the community and is supposed to use that authority accordingly. Restorative practices represent a huge paradigm shift in which staff confront behavior, but also share their own feelings as part of that process. Using a *with*-based approach, RAs make themselves vulnerable, express how the inappropriate behavior is impacting them and ask questions of residents to help them understand how their behavior is affecting others. Restorative practices put the emphasis on sustaining good relationships because ultimately that is more effective in achieving behavior change. While RAs may, at times, still have an obligation to "document" students, writing up and reporting their violations of residence hall regulations, they have moved beyond a strictly legalistic and punitive approach by allowing people to have a voice, to explain what happened and to share how they have been affected. This creates a more cordial and cooperative atmosphere in the residence halls.

Evidence

Criminal offenses on college campuses are primarily public disorder, petty theft, vandalism and other offenses associated with drug and alcohol use among young people. There is no evidence at UVM that the use of conferencing has reduced those crimes. However, there is a great deal of anecdotal evidence that the systematic use of restorative practices has provided RAs with viable strategies to address those offenses, resolve conflicts between roommates and hall neighbors, and deal with a wide range of incidents from lesser to serious. Before the advent of restorative practices, many of those incidents would have been left completely unresolved, with tensions and bad feelings persisting. Here are a few examples.

A male student on a co-ed floor was sleepwalking. On returning from the bathroom to his room, wearing only boxer shorts, he inadvertently entered a number of bedrooms occupied by women. The women were startled and frightened and believed they were potential victims of a sexual assault. As the man went from room to room, everyone finally realized that he was sleepwalking and couldn't find his own bed. Nonetheless, the next day a circle was convened so the women had an opportunity to explain what happened from their point of view, see the problem clearly and express their feelings about it. This process resolved the awkward feelings and lingering fears.

Another story told in the words of an RA: "One of our residents really enjoyed coming back from the gym very sweaty and then giving people big bear hugs. These people didn't really appreciate these sweaty bear hugs, so I used restorative practices to help facilitate a conversation between the hug receivers and the hugger."

Someone set a smoke bomb off in a carpeted hallway on a co-ed housing residential floor. The carpet caught on fire, triggering the fire alarms but fortunately not the sprinklers. The police were called and they questioned students about what happened. Some female students told the police they believed certain men on the hall may have been involved. The police questioned these men, who denied involvement and were angry at the women who accused them. They said they believed the incident should have been resolved internally without police involvement. The police left without making any arrests, but the incident left everyone on the floor with a lot of unresolved feelings.

The residential staff decided to convene a community circle for the residents. One of the strong themes that came up was that residents really liked their floor, and they didn't like the fact that someone had set off a smoke bomb there. Some people expressed their relief that the fire was minimal and hadn't set off the sprinklers, which would have caused major damage. The students who felt defensive about having been questioned by the campus police also had the chance to express how they felt. By the end of the meeting most of the bad feelings were diffused. People trusted that everyone was committed to seeing that things like this did not happen again, and they were able to move on with their lives.

An RA who was among the most resistant to using restorative practices went to her director exasperated about a group of students who were driving her crazy. She said that no matter what she did, the inappropriate behavior persisted. Most recently, over the weekend, she had written up discipline reports on nine students who were drinking alcohol in the residence hall.

Her director said, "Let's schedule a circle meeting with all those students" and assured her that if that didn't work, they might have to ask some of the students to move out of the residence hall. The director then facilitated a circle discussion with the students and the RA.

In the circle the director asked, "Why do you think we're having this conversation now?" The students acknowledged that it was because of the trouble they'd been causing on the hall and for having been written up for alcohol use. He then asked, "What impact do you think your behavior is having on the other residents and your RA?"

The students tried to answer this, but the biggest reaction came when the RA herself spoke. She said, "I don't even want to go to the back of the hallway because I'm afraid of all of you and what I'll find going on there." The residents were shocked. They said, "We like you, and we didn't want to have this impact." Afterward they said, "We appreciate being able to have this conversation and have a word with both of you rather than just being punished."

When the director followed up with the RA a few days later, she reported that things were better on the floor. The director reminded her that the expectation for the circle was not that it would make things perfect forever and that the RA would eventually deal with more issues with that group of students. Nonetheless, the RA, who had been known for her skeptical attitude toward restorative practices from the start, laughingly acknowledged, "Dammit, it worked again!"

During UVM's first year of restorative practices implementation, a student who lived in the residence halls committed suicide. RAs immediately recognized the healing power of circles for resident students who were shocked, saddened and deeply troubled by the incident.

There was a huge turnout at the first circle held that night, when 250 people gathered in the student union. Students received information that confirmed and clarified some of the rumors they'd been hearing, and they had a chance to express their grief and confusion about what was going on. The discussion was open for people to talk about their feelings and ask for more information, and some people began to talk about what they wanted to do next, in terms of memorializing the student, interacting with his parents and what to do with his belongings.

Over the next several nights, follow-up community circles were held throughout the residence halls. People checked in, and there were different needs expressed. Administrators felt the circle was a good format because there was no expectation of participation. People could show up to the meeting or not, and share what they needed to share or not share at all without being judged. Some students declined to speak or said, "I don't know how I feel." Some said, "This has really triggered some stuff, and I need to talk to the counseling staff later." The circle allowed for different reactions, and some floor communities spent more time processing their feelings than others. But because people already had familiarity with each other from previous routine circle meetings, they felt comfortable sharing their feelings. Although this was a highly emotional topic, RAs were also comfortable facilitating circle discussions because they already had some experience with the process.

Circles played an important part in the healing process. Another circle was held for each community a week later and then throughout the semester as needed to check in with residents. Follow-up circles were helpful for people who didn't know how to respond during the initial circle. Some students even said, "I don't know how I'm feeling," so the follow-up circles were helpful when they got in touch with their feelings and were able to share their reactions.

Circles were also used with RAs and for the entire residential staff. Circles gave staff in that residential complex an opportunity to share among themselves; staff from the counseling center also joined those circles. In fact, circles, while providing a known format, were flexible enough to allow not just communities but others to participate as well, without reconfiguring the whole group dynamic.

A key administrator commented, "Circles helped us move through the healing process of his death more than we would have been able to without them."

Although a growing number of higher education institutions are using restorative justice to respond to wrongdoing, to the best of our knowledge UVM is the only school, so far, that has undertaken implementation on such a large scale, including the whole range of proactive and responsive restorative practices in their residence halls. As a veteran of residential life and housing in higher education, Stacey Miller believes the advantages are compelling. When I asked her to summarize her experience with restorative practices, she wrote back to me:

> I had honestly given up hope that I or anyone in student affairs would ever find the tool that could truly build community or effectively address wrongdoing with students in residential settings. I became complacent. I believed that community-building was a haphazard process that some RAs and staff just could do better than others. I accepted the random chance of a good year versus a bad year. I would muddle through each year becoming more and more disillusioned with my profession and career. However, the persistence of a colleague and a happenstance meeting turned on the light bulb for me. Literally, in one

demonstration of the circle process I had a professional epiphany. I could see all the connections between theory and practice and how restorative practices could be a game changer.

Now in our third full year of implementation I can honestly say that we are more effective in our work with students and each other. Restorative practices provide a highly structured and accessible framework to lead, to connect students with one another and, in difficult times, to address problematic behavior. Restorative practices are easy to do, but challenging to implement because they go against our fundamental and socialized perceptions about how people change their behavior. By the time we are 18, 19 or 20, the age of our RAs, we are fully acculturated and wholeheartedly believe in justice by punishment. But we have forgotten the need to address the pain that wrongdoing and injustice imposes on a victim and a community.

Our restorative practices approach builds community, addresses harm, still allows for sanctions and other punitive consequences — but has the power to reestablish relationships, which on a college campus is fundamental to every student's success. I cannot yet provide the empirical data, but the sustained culture shift we have witnessed on our campus is evidence enough.

Restorative Works

Chapter 8
Restorative Works

We are doing more than dreaming of a new reality. We are building it.

Following the advice of Henry David Thoreau, quoted in my 1977 slide show, the IIRP has "put the foundations under" its "castles in the air." We have gained experience, achieved positive outcomes and built infrastructure to promote restorative practices across professional disciplines and national boundaries.

In the previous chapters I described six areas of endeavor in which the IIRP and its affiliates have had successful experiences in using restorative practices:

> - with delinquent and at-risk youth, improving social attitudes and reducing re-offending;
> - in public and private schools, reducing violence, crime, bullying and misbehavior;
> - in criminal justice, coping with the emotional consequences of crime, reducing re-offending and diverting young offenders from the courts;
> - with families, in social services and criminal justice, helping them manage their own problems more effectively;
> - in workplaces, improving morale and personal accountability;
> - in higher education, increasing cooperation and improving relationships in residential life.

Worldwide Innovation

Besides the IIRP, there are many others around the world who are exploring the application of restorative justice and other restorative practices in a variety of settings. Here is a notably incomplete sampling of those activities:

> in faith communities, using circles and restorative conferences to resolve conflicts in congregations or using the circle format, rather than Robert's Rules of Order, to ensure that everyone's voice is heard at meetings;[89]

> in classrooms, using circles, not only to enhance relationships and resolve conflicts, but as a pedagogical strategy to enhance teaching and learning;[90]

> with at-risk families, encouraging young mothers and improving their child-rearing skills;[91]

> in residential child care agencies, refining staff skills and improving long-term outcomes for the children;[92]

> with victimized children, helping them overcome trauma;[93]

> with domestic or intimate relationship violence, using restorative justice to address abusive behaviors, assure safety and, where appropriate, restore relationships;[94]

> in prisons, working with inmates to learn new skills, reconnect with loved ones and prepare for life outside prison;[95]

> within a maximum security prison, painting a mural to display in the outside community about "healing from crime" involving inmates, victims of crime and a neighborhood group in a collaborative process;[96]

> with politically motivated prisoners, engaging them in speaking openly about their actions, motivations and effects on victims and survivors and their plans to desist from violence in the future;[97]

> in a prison without employees, running the institution with community volunteers and restorative processes;[98]

> in county jails, confronting violence with restorative justice strategies;[99]

> with sex offenders released from prison, using community volunteers to create "circles of support and accountability" to prevent re-offending;[100]

> ➤ with neighborhood conflicts, using restorative confer-
> ences to engage people in developing a plan to solve the
> problem;[101]
> ➤ in intercultural settings, handling conflicts involving
> communities with people from different cultural
> backgrounds;[102]
> ➤ in low income neighborhoods in developing countries,
> working with residents to resolve conflicts using circles and
> other restorative practices;[103]
> ➤ in response to a case of industrial pollution of a river, using a
> restorative justice forum to resolve the issues quickly, as an
> alternative to years of delay and extended court trials.[104]

All of these innovative approaches rely on the same fundamental premise — that it is better to do things *with* people, than *to* them or *for* them. As those in authority recognize the merits of giving people an opportunity to be heard and engaging them in dealing with their own problems, the possibilities seem limitless. Restorative practitioners, to their credit, have not shied away from difficult issues. In fact, they have taken on and made headway with some of the greatest challenges facing humanity, demonstrating a courageous spirit that inspires hope.

Restorative Zones: Expanding the Restorative Milieu

The IIRP has also taken on difficult challenges — in particular, how to curb misbehavior, bullying, violence and crime among young people. From its origins in the CSF Buxmont schools, the IIRP's strategies have shown great promise. Now the IIRP is attempting to take restorative practices to scale — implementing restorative practices in "school-based restorative zones."

The restorative zone concept has evolved from the restorative milieu of the CSF Buxmont schools. Paul McCold first used the term "restorative milieu" to describe the environment found at CSF Buxmont when reporting the findings of his empirical evaluation of those programs. He determined that spending a few months in the program setting, where everyone used restorative practices all day long, reduced criminal offending by more than half and improved social attitudes and program completion rates.[105]

McCold's findings lent credence to my own advocacy for "Restorative Justice in Everyday Life: Beyond the Formal Process," which I first presented at an academic conference in 1999.[106] At that time I was concerned that restorative justice practitioners were unrealistic in hoping for significant behavioral change in offenders who had only participated in a single restorative justice event, such as a victim-offender mediation or a restorative conference. I suggested that an environment where a range of informal and formal restorative interventions were used continuously, day after day, would be more likely to produce reductions in antisocial behavior. The idea of a restorative milieu, rather than merely a single intervention for each incident of wrongdoing, proved to have merit.

Having started my professional life as a schoolteacher, I had long held that public and private schools could benefit from the strategies we were using in our CSF Buxmont programs. However, it was not until the 1998–99 school year, when Joseph Roy became the first school principal to take us up on our offer of training his staff in restorative practices, that we had an opportunity to put the idea to the test. By creating a restorative milieu in an entire school, Palisades High School experienced improved school climate and reduced disciplinary incidents, suspensions and expulsions. Similar implementation of restorative practices in many rural, suburban and urban schools in Canada, the U.S. and the U.K. has achieved favorable outcomes.[107]

The expansion of the restorative milieu from the school itself into neighborhoods around the school was the next stage in the progression of our thinking. The "restorative zone" relies on the positive changes in school climate, which provide a springboard for each school to reach beyond its walls to partner with parents, police, faith-based organizations, social services, juvenile probation and other agencies to foster a restorative environment in the communities surrounding the school. These stakeholders, in their own spheres of influence and in cooperation with one another, develop capacity to respond to harm in a restorative manner that holds youth accountable while supporting them in making positive changes.

In 2007 an opportunity to create a school-based restorative zone arose when the IIRP began working in Hull, England, a city of a quarter-million residents that in 2005 the BBC named the "worst place to live in the U.K." The initial focus was on Riverside, Hull's most economically deprived area, although the long-term intention was to make Hull the "first restorative city." Schools in Hull that embraced restorative practices reported reductions in classroom disruption of as much as 90 percent. Police and youth justice officials reported that youth re-offending in the city declined to only 13 percent, compared to a 27 percent national average, and that custodial sentencing (incarceration) was down by 23 percent.[108] There were other restorative initiatives in services for at-risk children and families in Hull.

The IIRP gave Hull considerable attention in its publications and at its conferences, holding our 13th international conference there in 2010. Others, from Lima, Peru, to Detroit, Michigan, to Wanganui, New Zealand, to Nova Scotia, Canada, where we held our 14th international conference in 2011, also have taken steps toward creating a restorative zone or restorative city or restorative province — a noble aspiration but a difficult one to achieve.

Strengthening Implementation

The obstacles to meaningful implementation are formidable. The IIRP has gradually adjusted and enhanced its tactics as it has acquired experience.

First, we want to ensure high-quality restorative practice among a high percentage of an organization's staff. We now recommend that initial trainings be followed by on-site consultation with our staff, professional learning groups and participatory self-evaluation based on a set of explicit "essential elements" that help staff recognize what good restorative practice looks like and when they are doing it reliably.[109] We also collaborate with Anne Gregory, a Rutgers University professor whose research group has created an observational tool to evaluate restorative circles and conferences.[110]

Second, we want to achieve sustainability. We train members of the organization's staff at each implementation site, who are then authorized to use the IIRP's copyrighted training materials to teach restorative practices to new staff as they are hired. The biggest obstacle to sustainability is change in leadership, especially in governmental organizations where administrative turnover is more frequent. Few successors are willing to sustain the previous leader's initiatives, usually because they want to put their own imprint on the organization.

For that reason, in our evolving approach to organizational change, we are seeking to develop grassroots support among the organization's constituency. The school-based restorative zone, for example, has the potential to embed restorative practices in the hearts and minds of staff, students and community members, so that a new school administrator cannot easily abandon the use of restorative practices. We strive to make restorative practices integral to everyone's expectations and behavior.

Third, we try to connect everyone we train with the growing restorative practices social movement, so they feel part of something larger than what is happening in their own organization. During our first decade of trainings, more than 35,000 people subscribed to our Restorative Practices eForum, a free news Internet publication that is now part of our "Restorative Works" learning network. Sponsored by the Restorative Practices Foundation, the IIRP's philanthropic sister organization, the restorativeworks.net website features news, articles, book reviews, interviews and videos focusing on "what works, what doesn't, how and why" from around the world.

Rarely does a social movement come with such a compelling track record and relate to so many aspects of our lives. Yet the emerging field of restorative practices has only begun the research necessary to create a mature social science. Not only must we find opportunities and funding to conduct randomized control trials, the highest standard of empirical evaluation, to further demonstrate the efficacy of restorative strategies, but we must also investigate and identify what makes good practice and how to measure it.

Fourth, we want to provide educational experiences of the highest caliber in conjunction with our implementation efforts. The IIRP's professional development events can also be applied toward graduate coursework in its master's degree and graduate certificate programs. When the Pennsylvania Department of Education and the Middle States Commission on Higher Education authorized and accredited the IIRP, they not only certified a new specialized educational and research institution, but they acknowledged restorative practices as a social science worthy of graduate study. Post-baccalaureate studies help professionals understand restorative practices at a much deeper level, still another way of strengthening implementation.

A New Reality

To reach those people who hold strong beliefs about punishment and authoritarian management strategies, despite a growing body of evidence that contradicts those beliefs, we will need more than research results to win their understanding and support. We must address their underlying preferences and point out the benefits to them personally. For those on the political and philosophical left, for example, the appeal of restorative practices may be that they provide effective means to help people in need. For those on the right, we may appeal to their concern about undue dependence on government, because restorative practices encourage individuals and families to take greater responsibility for their own problems. Ultimately, the most effective persuasion is inherent in the power of restorative practices to create a new reality in our daily lives.

The *Code of the Street*[111] dominates the lives of inner-city youth. Commenting on ethnographer Elijah Anderson's important book by that name, *Washington Post* reviewer Jonathan Yardley wrote, "Violence in the inner city is regulated through an informal but well-known code of the street. How you dress, talk, and behave can have life-or-death consequences, with young people particularly at risk. ... Unfortunately, the culture of the street thrives and often defeats decency because it controls public spaces, so that individuals with higher, better aspirations are often entangled in the code and its self-destructive behaviors."[112]

The story from earlier in this book about the transformation of West Philadelphia High School, where restorative circles liberated students from daily fear and violence, and the story entitled "Somebody could have died that day," in which a ninth-grade student used a circle process to stop a fight in a Detroit high school, both suggest that restorative practices can be an effective antidote to the "code of the streets." This potential is further illustrated in another IIRP blog post, "Using Their Words Instead of Their Fists,"[113] in which Winston Alozie, program director of the Boys & Girls Clubs of Bethlehem, tells this story:

> I was in the Bethlehem Area School District Superintendent's Committee on Diversity meeting, and people were discussing how restorative practices are working in the district. There had been a year of restorative practices implementation at Liberty and Freedom high schools in Bethlehem at this time. The NAACP was in on the meeting, too, and they were asking, "Does it work?" When I heard this, I was eager to share how I had seen the practices working outside the classroom.
>
> We have a large gymnasium where I see 80 to 100 kids a day, mostly high school students. They love to play basketball. One afternoon I walked into the gym and the kids were on the verge of a fight. Boys were pushing and yelling — taking sides and gathering around two boys in the center. Some of these kids have gang affiliations, so I was afraid this could be bad. But what could have turned into a big brouhaha did not because the kids used restorative practices.

One boy was offended by what another boy had said to him. They were yelling back and forth, when one boy suddenly said, "Look, I don't want to fight. I don't like what you said; you hurt my feelings." Then the other boy said, "You're right. I'm sorry. I didn't mean to hurt your feelings. Let's not do this."

I was so proud of these kids: that high school students could behave that way. One kid was able to say how the other kid had affected him, and the other kid was able to take responsibility and apologize. They weren't afraid of being seen as a wimp or less of a man. And there was nobody standing over them and telling them to do this; it was their own idea.

It was clear to me they had learned how to do this from the restorative practices and circles they had learned at Liberty. These kids are learning how to be compassionate and empathetic, how to be in touch with their feelings and the feelings of others. I had never seen anything like this in nine years working at the Boys & Girls Clubs.

I have my bachelor's degree in developmental psychology. When I first heard about restorative practices I thought, OK, but how's it going to work with regular kids? When I saw what those boys did it really touched me. If you can express yourself effectively with words, it's a beautiful thing. I hope we can incorporate these practices into the Boys & Girls Clubs. I think it would help us with our mission to help our kids reach their full potential as productive, caring, responsible citizens.

The story suggests that as people learn about the value of restorative practices in one setting, they intuitively bring it to another. Although less dramatic than preventing violence, yet equally important to the reality of our daily lives, are the challenges of parenting. Aimee Lewis Strain, in an online article, wrote about her first experience in using restorative practices rather than punishment. She was driving home from an amusement park after an altercation with her young son about having to share a bag of cotton candy with his siblings. She had recently read about several San Francisco schools that were using the IIRP's restorative practices strategies to reduce suspensions and expulsions.

But I couldn't shake the idea that my son is being sent to his room for bad-mouthing me in the cotton candy incident. It seemed very much like suspension in a school environment. [Am I] sending a 7-year-old to his room to reflect on his actions ... or play with the million toys in there that line the walls? Suspension in a school environment might seem like a day off to some too. Do these methods really force the individual to focus at all on the conflict? Do these methods offer any valid reflection?

We got home after our hour-long ride from Gilroy, my mind racing with this whole restorative practices idea. The three kids jumped out of the car — two from their cotton candy buzz — and ran inside. My oldest son was nearing his room when I asked him to join me at the dining room table. He looked at me blankly and reminded me of his time out. (An easy form of punishment, I now realized.)

Instead of sending my son away for a 20-minute time out, I chose to talk to him about his actions. Following the model I briefly read about, together we identified new solutions, talked of his lack of cotton candy and then moved on. But it felt good. I actually feel like he understood why he was denied cotton candy and he felt it was a fair thing for me to do based on his behavior.[114]

A former student in our CSF Buxmont schools reported that he had gone to his boss to suggest holding a circle to deal with conflicts that were disrupting their workplace. His boss agreed and was surprised and pleased by the successful outcome. The adverse issues were addressed and resolved, and everyone enjoyed the positive atmosphere that ensued.

Mary Schott, a 2010 graduate of the IIRP master's degree program, explained how restorative practices created a new reality for her and her primary school students:

> After using time outs or taking a child to the office for misbehaving, I used to go home from work and I had the feeling that something just wasn't right. The kids had no say. Especially teaching primary children as I do, where you spend so much time trying to develop their emerging social skills and their emerging independence and communication. It just seemed counterproductive. But once I started using restorative practices, things actually felt good. Conflicts became resolved in a fair and respectful way. And it turned out that the kids with the most behavior problems made the biggest change.[115]

Restorative practices offer more than a discipline strategy or an approach to conflict resolution. They foster a way of behaving and interacting with our fellow human beings. Marsha Walker, a 2011 graduate of the IIRP master's degree program and one of the teachers who participated in the transformation of West Philadelphia High School, exclaimed, "Restorative practices to me is like a way of life."[116]

When children and adults are actively engaged in the issues that matter to them, when they feel their voices are truly heard, when they feel a sense of belonging to a group, they internalize a commitment to the others in that group that reduces the likelihood of conflict and misbehavior — but that also feels good and makes for positive relationships.

Even in prisons, now ruled largely through hierarchy, regimentation and a demand for obedience, there are those who are thinking about and experimenting with training correctional officers in restorative ways of responding to wrongdoing and teaching inmates how to facilitate restorative circles to resolve conflicts.[117] Several years ago I was pleasantly surprised to find a governor of a prison attending a basic restorative practices training I was offering in Manchester, U.K.

Might the same kind of restorative milieu that CSF Buxmont has successfully employed with adolescents to reduce drug abuse and re-offending also be helpful with adults in prisons and halfway houses? Might corrections, probation and parole officers find that restorative practices can improve their outcomes with offenders?

Others have experimented with a variety of restorative practices in the aftermath of violent conflicts: a truth and reconciliation commission in South Africa,[118] dispute resolution in Rwanda[119] and peacemaking circles in New Guinea.[120] Might the use of restorative practices reduce the chance of civil unrest and violence in the future?

For those skeptics who snicker and scoff at such aspirations, we need only to remind them that there have been skeptics throughout history. They could not envision an end to monarchy nor slavery nor women having the right to vote nor homosexuals having the right to marry. Human culture, whether we like it or not, changes in ways that we may find hard to imagine.

In terms of restorative practices, we have only begun to explore the possibilities of a new reality.

Restorative Practices and Democratic Citizenship

While people have different perceptions of what is wrong in the world and varied solutions and priorities, restorative practices stand on the common ground. We are all social creatures with a universal need to feel connected to others. Sadly, democracy increasingly fails to provide that sense of belonging. Once the great hope of humanity, many democratic endeavors around the world have been co-opted and become facades that camouflage the greed and manipulation of dictators. Even established democracies have devolved into systems of governance that are often divisive and ineffectual.

"The lived experience of modern democracy is alienation. The feeling is that elites run things, that we do not have a say in any meaningful sense," exclaimed John Braithwaite at the IIRP's second world conference in 1999. "Circles and conferences, in contrast, teach active responsibility."[121]

Human beings' earliest discussions were held in circles around the fire. Somewhere along the way as our numbers grew and our social organizations became more complex, we moved out of egalitarian circles into hierarchical structures. Now, often from a raised platform, leaders typically face others seated in rows, with most of the group looking at the backs of the people in front of them.[122]

Yet, in a variety of settings and for a variety of purposes, we are rediscovering the power of circles. For all our technological advances, we have come to realize that we lost something along the way — a very simple and effective technology that fosters mutual understanding and healing in a way that often seems magical.[123]

In circles we face each other and speak respectfully, one person at a time, allowing the quiet voices to be heard, diminishing the feeling of disconnectedness that permeates our modern world and restoring the sense of belongingness that constitutes healthy human community. We may find that this ancient form of social discourse helps us address our greatest challenges.[124]

Restorative practices have the potential to bring us together, to guide those in authority toward a more participatory approach to solving problems, to foster a new understanding of democratic citizenship. Restorative practices can influence the evolution of the role of government — moving us beyond relying unduly on government to solve our problems, while engaging us in dealing more directly with the issues that concern us.

Restoring Community in a Disconnected World

From the founding of the United States, when more than 90 percent of us worked on farms to less than 3 percent of us at present (there are similar trends in every country), technology has transformed our nation and our world. My 98-year-old father remembers the crackling sounds of the first radio broadcasts, the first refrigerators, the first commercial airlines and as a soldier expecting to participate in the invasion of Japan, the first use of nuclear weapons. Driven by technological change, family farms, neighborhood stores and local factories have given way to agribusiness, national discount store chains, fast-food franchises and multinational corporations. Globalization and the relentless growth of government have dramatically altered our lives.

William Irwin Thompson wrote, "At the edge of history the future is blowing wildly in our faces, sometimes brightening the air and sometimes blinding us." He said, "In straining our industrial technology to the limit, we have, in fact, reached the limit of that very technology. Now as we stand in the shadow of our success, there remains light enough to see that we are approaching a climax in human cultural evolution."[125]

I am not a doomsday prophet and I know that we cannot turn back the clock. Rather, we must find ways to adapt and to compensate for our profound loss of social connectedness. And I know that restorative practices can play a critical role in doing just that — in restoring community and fostering relationships in an increasingly disconnected world.

But to do so, we must now thoughtfully re-examine and change many of the practices that govern how our modern societies run schools, administer justice, organize social welfare systems and manage workplaces, and even how we raise children.

The modern restorative justice movement was initiated by probation officers who were experimenting with meetings between victims and offenders to negotiate restitution agreements. They learned that the encounter was more important than the restitution — that both victims and offenders valued the opportunity to talk to each other and resolve their conflicts. [126]

Years ago I was speaking about restorative conferencing to an audience in Philadelphia, Pennsylvania, when a woman from Africa said: "What you're describing is exactly what my father would do. As a traditional chief, he would always bring everyone together to deal with a crime or a conflict."

Bonnie George, of the Wet'suwet'en First Nation in British Columbia, Canada, was a plenary speaker at our conference in

Vancouver. She contrasted her people's indigenous justice system with the adversarial Western system in which strangers make decisions on behalf of others, without emotional involvement. She said, "With our system because of our relationships and our kinships, we're all connected to each other one way or another, and those are the people that are making the decisions. Our goal is to restore balance and harmony within the community."[127] So if restorative practices are the wave of the future, we may take comfort in knowing that they are also as old as the hills.

We must not be embarrassed by our optimism. The world needs our vision of hope. The human race now holds in its mortal hands the power to tinker with the genetic underpinnings of life, to alter the climate of our planet, to extinguish whole species and to wield, as weaponry, the awesome energy of the stars. Our technological skills have outpaced our social skills, but restorative practices can correct that imbalance.

No, we are not pursuing an unrealistic utopian dream. We recognize that conflict is integral to being human. What we propose, however, is to get better at managing conflict. And to minimize conflict by proactively restoring community in a disconnected world.

Join us.

Postscript

The International Institute for Restorative Practices (IIRP) is the first higher education institution wholly dedicated to restorative practices. We offer professional development events that provide practical support to those trying to understand and implement restorative practices. Those professional development events are modules in a larger educational framework and may be applied toward academic credit by supplementing them with online coursework.

The IIRP offers master's degrees and graduate certificates in restorative practices. Our Master of Science in Restorative Practices degree program is available from anywhere in the world. The degree program is comprised of mostly online and independent study combined with a variety of face-to-face professional development experiences. We rely on our network of licensees and affiliates to build local capacity, making restorative practices education affordable and accessible at a growing number of locations.

We collaborate with other institutions to conduct and disseminate research. We distribute and produce films, publish books and organize multidisciplinary international conferences.

We maintain numerous websites:

> *restorativeworks.net* is our learning network website. You may register for a free subscription to the Restorative Practices eForum, the "voice" of Restorative Works. The eForum provides news and announcements. Subscribing is an easy first step to learning more about restorative practices and joining this hopeful social movement;

> *iirp.edu* is dedicated to our graduate school and professional development division;
> *csfbuxmont.org* describes our schools, group homes and other programs for delinquent and at-risk youth;
> *safersanerschools.org* highlights our Whole-School Change program and our efforts to improve school climate;
> *realjustice.org* describes our efforts to produce better outcomes for offenders and victims in the criminal justice system;
> *familypower.org* features family group conferencing or family group decision making and other programs that empower families;
> *goodcompanyonline.org* focuses on how to improve leadership, workplace satisfaction and productivity through restorative practices;
> *buildingcampuscommunity.org* features the use of restorative practices in residential settings and campus life in higher education;
> *restorativepracticesfoundation.org* is dedicated to the IIRP's philanthropic sister organization, which helps to bring restorative practices education to worthy students, disadvantaged communities and developing countries.

IIRP Consortium of Organizations

The IIRP has demonstration programs that for many years have provided restorative practices for delinquent and at-risk youth in eastern Pennsylvania, as well as a network of affiliates and licensees offering professional development around the world. The Restorative Practices Foundation assists worthy individuals and disadvantaged communities in affording professional development and graduate studies.

INTERNATIONAL INSTITUTE FOR RESTORATIVE PRACTICES *Graduate school* iirp.edu	**RESTORATIVE PRACTICES FOUNDATION** *Philanthropic support* restorativepracticesfoundation.org
BUXMONT ACADEMY *Educational services for troubled youth* csfbuxmont.org	**IIRP AFFILIATES** *Professional development* *— regional partners —* iirp.edu/affiliates.php
COMMUNITY SERVICE FOUNDATION *Counseling and residential services for youth* csfbuxmont.org	**IIRP LICENSEES** *Professional development* *— local providers —*

Endnotes

Endnotes

1   Lennon, J. & McCartney, P. (1970). Let it be. On *Let It Be*. London: Apple Records.

2   Sandburg, C. (1922). Washington Monument by Night. In *Slabs of the Sunburnt West*. New York: Harcourt, Brace & Company.

3   Thoreau, H. D. (1854). *Walden*. Boston, MA: Ticknor & Fields.

4   http://www.csfbuxmont.org

5   Cohen, D. & Prusak, L. (2001). *In Good Company: How Social Capital Makes Organizations Work*. Boston, MA: Harvard Business School Press.

6   Wachtel, T. (2012). Defining restorative. Retrieved from http://www.iirp.edu/what-is-restorative-practices.php

7   http://www.csfbuxmont.org

8   http://www.iirp.edu

9   Wachtel, T. (2012, September 27). A shift away from zero tolerance will improve school discipline. *Christian Science Monitor*. Retrieved from http://www.csmonitor.com/Commentary/Opinion/2012/0927/A-shift-away-from-zero-tolerance-will-improve-school-discipline-video

10   International Institute for Restorative Practices (Producer). (2008). *Beyond Zero Tolerance: Restorative Practices in Schools* [25-minute DVD]. Bethlehem, PA. Available from http://www.iirp.edu/books_n_videos.php

11   Esack, S. (2012, September 12). Discipline infractions drop at Liberty and Freedom high schools. Allentown, PA: *Morning Call*.

Retrieved from http://articles.mcall.com/2012-09-12/news/mc-bethlehem-schools-912-20120912_1_high-schools-expulsion-hearings-superintendent-joseph-roy

12 From data provided by Bethlehem Area School District to IIRP.

13 Adapted from the Vision presented on the Eigen Kracht Centrale website. Retrieved from http://www.eigen-kracht.nl/en/inhoud/what-we-do

14 From the mission statement of the IIRP. Retrieved from http://www.iirp.edu/mission-vision.php

15 Kim, W. C., & Mauborgne, R. (1997). Fair process: Managing in the knowledge economy. *Harvard Business Review*, July-August. 65-75.

16 Ibid.

17 Thibaut, J. & Walker, W. (1975). *Procedural Justice: A Psychological Analysis*. Hillsdale, NJ: Laurence Erbaum Associates. As cited in Sanders, J. & Hamilton V.L. (Eds.) (2001) *Handbook of Justice Research in Law*. New York: Kluwer Academic/Plenum Publishers. 70.

18 O'Connell, T. The restorative questions were developed in 1991 by O'Connell, a former police officer from Australia who is one of the pioneers of restorative justice and who has served as the director of Real Justice Australia, an IIRP affiliate.

19 http://www.iirp.edu/oscommerce-2.3.1/catalog/index.php?cPath=62

20 McCold, P. (2002). Evaluation of a restorative milieu: CSF Buxmont school/day treatment programs 1999-2001, Evaluation outcome technical report. Bethlehem, PA: International Institute for Restorative Practices. Retrieved from http://www.iirp.edu/article_detail.php?article_id=NDM5

McCold, P. (2005). Evaluation of a restorative milieu: Replication and extension for 2001-2003 discharges. Bethlehem, PA.

International Institute for Restorative Practices: Bethlehem, Pennsylvania. Retrieved from http://www.iirp.edu/article_ detail.php?article_id=Mzky

21 McCold, P. & Wachtel T. (2001). Restorative justice in everyday life. In Strang, H. & Braithwaite, J., (Eds.), *Restorative Justice and Civil Society* (pp. 114-129). Cambridge: Cambridge University Press.

22 Ibid. 125-126.

23 Ibid. 126.

24 Ibid. 126.

25 Tomkins, S. (1962). *Affect Imagery Consciousness, Vol. I.* New York: Springer.

Tomkins, S. (1963). *Affect Imagery Consciousness, Vol. II.* New York: Springer.

Tomkins, S. (1991). *Affect Imagery Consciousness, Vol. III.* New York: Springer.

26 Nathanson, D. (1998, August). *From empathy to community.* Paper presented at Conferencing: A New Response to Wrongdoing, The First North American Conference on Conferencing, Minneapolis, MN. Retrieved from http://www.iirp.edu/article_ detail.php?article_id=NDg3

27 Tomkins, S. (1962, 1963, 1991). Op cit.

28 Tomkins, S. (1987). Shame. In Nathanson, D. (Ed.), *The Many Faces of Shame* (pp. 133-161). New York: Norton.

29 Nathanson, D. (1997). Affect theory and the compass of shame. In M. Lansky and Morrison, A. (Eds.), *The Widening Scope of Shame.* Hillsdale, NJ: The Analytic Press, Inc.

30 Nathanson, D. (1992). *Shame and Pride: Affect, Sex, and the Birth of the Self.* New York: Norton.

31 Nathanson, D. (1992). Op. cit.

[32] Nathanson, D. (1998). Op. cit.

[33] Cassidy, T. (2007). In a videotaped interview for the CSF Buxmont website. Retrieved from http://www.csfbuxmont.org/testimonials.php

[34] McCold, P. (2002). Op. cit. 14.

[35] McCold, P. (2005). Op. cit. 1.

[36] Ibid. 6.

[37] McCold, P. & Chang, A. (2008). Community Service Foundation and Buxmont Academy analysis of students discharged during three school years (2003-2006). Bethlehem, PA: International Institute for Restorative Practices. Retrieved from http://www.iirp.edu/article_detail.php?article_id=NTc2

[38] None of these evaluations were randomized control trials. Aside from any ethical considerations related to assigning individuals to a control group, courts and schools do not send young people to participate in programs they consider less effective than others, so other research methodology had to be employed.

[39] http://www. safersanerschools.org

[40] *Beyond Zero Tolerance*. Op. cit.

[41] American Psychological Association, Task Force on Zero Tolerance. (2008). Are zero tolerance policies effective in the schools? An evidentiary review and recommendations. *American Psychologist*, 63(9), 858-862.

[42] McNeely, C.A., Nonnemaker, J.M. & Blum, R.W. (2002). Promoting school connectedness: Evidence from the National Longitudinal Study of Adolescent Health, *Journal of School Health, 72(4)*, 138-146.

[43] Ibid. 145.

[44] International Institute for Restorative Practices (Producer). (2009). *The Transformation of West Philadelphia High School: A*

Story of Hope. [Nine-minute DVD]. A link to a YouTube video is available at http://www.safersanerschools.org.

45   Mirsky, L. (2011). Restorative practices: Giving everyone a voice to create safer saner school communities, *Prevention Researcher,* 18 (supplement) December. 3-6.

46   Ibid. 5.

47   Lewis, S. (2009). *Improving School Climate: Findings from Schools Implementing Restorative Practices.* Bethlehem, PA: International Institute for Restorative Practices. A link to a PDF of the report is available on the main webpage of safersanerschools.org.

48   Mirsky, L. (2011). Somebody could have died that day. *Restorative Practices eForum.* Bethlehem, PA: International Institute for Restorative Practices. Retrieved from http://blog.iirp. edu/2011/11/somebody-could-have-died-that-day

49   Cameron, D. (Producer), & Ziegler, A. (Director). (1999). *Facing the Demons.* Australia: Australian Film Finance Corporation. [60-minute DVD]: Available from http://www.iirp.edu/ books_n_videos.php

50   Porter, A. J. (2006). The Jerry Lee Program research on restorative justice: Promising results. *Restorative Practices eForum.* Bethlehem, PA: International Institute for Restorative Practices. Retrieved from http://www.iirp.edu/article_detail.php?article_id=NTMz

51   Christie, N. (1977). Conflicts as property. *The British Journal of Criminology.* 17 (1): 1-15.

52   Zehr, H. (1990). *Changing Lenses: A New Focus for Crime and Justice.* Scottdale, PA: Herald Press.

53   Wachtel, T. (1998). *Real Justice.* Pipersville, PA: Piper's Press.

54   *Conferencing for Serious Offenses: An Exploration.* (2006). 5 DVDs plus CD-ROM. Bethlehem, PA: International Institute for Restorative Practices. Available from http://www.iirp.edu/ books_n_videos.php

55 Walters, A. (2009, June 19). Father greets son's killer with unforgiveable forgiveness. Sydney, Australia: *The Daily Telegraph*.

56 Toy, N. & Walters, A. (2009, August 12). Michael Marslew's mother cannot forgive her son's killers. Sydney, Australia: *The Daily Telegraph*.

57 Jacobsen, G. & Welch, D. (2010, January 30). Forgiven killer in jail after months of freedom. Sydney, Australia: *The Sydney Morning Herald*.

58 Wachtel, T. (1998). Op. cit. 53-54.

59 Sherman, L. & Strang, H. (2007). *Restorative Justice: The Evidence*. London: Smith Institute.

60 Smith, N. & Weatherburn, D. (2012). Youth justice conferences versus children's court: A comparison of re-offending. *Crime and Justice Bulletin*. No. 160. Sydney, Australia: New South Wales Bureau of Crime Statistics and Research.

61 Sherman, L. & Strang, H. Op. cit.

62 Porter, A. J. (2006). Restorative Practices reduce trauma from crime, study shows. *Restorative Practices eForum*. Bethlehem, PA: International Institute for Restorative Practices. Retrieved from http://www.iirp.edu/article_detail.php?article_id=NTM2

63 Much of this chapter is from Smull, B., Wachtel, J. & Wachtel, T. (2012) *Family Power: Engaging and Collaborating with Families*. Bethlehem, PA: International Institute for Restorative Practices.

64 Burford, G. & Pennell, J. Family group decision making and family violence. In Burford, G. & Hudson, J. (Eds.), (2000). *Family group conferencing: New directions in community-centered child and family practice*. New York: Aldine De Gruyter. 171-183.

65 Merkel-Holguin, L. (2005). FGDM: An Evidence-based decision-making process in child welfare. *Protecting Children*. Vol. 10, No. 4. Englewood, CO: American Humane Association. 2-3.

[66] Barnsdale, L. & Walker, M. (2006). Examining the use and impact of family group conferencing: Executive summary. Edinburgh, Scotland: Scottish Executive. Retrieved from http://www.scotland.gov.uk/Publications/2007/03/26093721/2

[67] Eigen Kracht. (2004-2009). Results and cost benefits. From Dutch studies done by various research bureaus and varying in framework and scale. Retrieved from http://www.eigen-kracht.nl/en/inhoud/research

[68] Op. cit.

[69] International Institute for Restorative Practices (Producer). (2007). *Toxic Talk: From Betrayal to Trust in a Workplace.* [22-minute DVD]. Available from http://www.iirp.edu/books_n_videos.php

[70] Ibid.

[71] Kim, W. C. & Mauborgne, R. Op. cit. 66.

[72] Ibid. 72.

[73] Redeker, J. R. (1989). *Employee Discipline: Policies and Practices.* Washington, DC: The Bureau of National Affairs, Inc.

Taylor, F. W. (1911). *The Principles of Scientific Management.* New York and London: Harper & Brothers.

Weber, M. (1922). *Economy and Society,* Germany. Contemporary edition: Roth, G. & Wittich, C. (Eds.) (1978). Berkeley, CA: University of California Press.

[74] Blanchard, K. & Johnson, S. (1982). *One Minute Manager.* New York: William Morrow and Company.

[75] Quality Circles. *Inc. Magazine.* Retrieved from http://www.inc.com/encyclopedia/quality-circles.html

[76] Robbins, H. & Finley M. (2000). *Why The New Teams Don't Work: What Goes Wrong and How to Make It Right.* San Francisco; Berrett-Koehler Publishers, Inc. 258-9.

77 Cohen, D. & Prusak, L. (2001). *In Good Company: How Social Capital Makes Organizations Work*. Boston, MA: Harvard Business School Press.

78 Frazier, I. (2012, February 6). Out of the Bronx. *The New Yorker*, 58.

79 Kim, W. C. & Mauborgne, R. op. cit. 69.

80 Op. cit. 68.

81 Ibid.

82 Groysberg, B. & Slind, M. (2012). Leadership is a conversation. *Harvard Business Review*, June. Reprint. 3-4.

83 Op. cit, 5-10.

84 Hull, D., & Read, V. (2003). Simply the best workplaces in Australia. Working Paper 88. Sydney, Australia: Australian Centre for Industrial Relations Research and Training, University of Sydney.

85 Op. cit. 12.

86 Adapted from chapter by Miller, S., & Wachtel, T. (2011). Looking for the Magic, as well as selected stories from other chapters from in Wachtel, J., & Wachtel, T. (2011). *Building Campus Community*. Bethlehem, PA: International Institute for Restorative Practices.

87 Astin, A.W. (1993). *What matters in college? Four critical years revisited*. San Francisco, CA: Jossey-Bass.

88 Piper, T. (1996, November). The community standards model: A method to enhance student learning and development. *ACUHO-I Talking Stick*. 14-15.

89 Wachtel, J. (2012) FaithCARE: Creating restorative congregations. *Restorative Practices eForum*. Bethlehem, PA: International Institute for Restorative Practices. Retrieved from: http://www.iirp.edu/article_detail.php?article_id=NzEx

90 McCormick, P. J. (2012, August). *Teaching and learning in circles: Building community, developing relationships and enhancing*

learning—mission possible? Presentation at Building a Restorative Practices Learning Network, IIRP 15th World Conference, Bethlehem, PA.

91 Mast, S. (2013). Baby college: Restorative practices help build a future with at-risk families. *Restorative Works Learning Network.* Retrieved from http://restorativeworks.net/2013/04/baby-college/

92 Negrea, V. In private email to Ted Wachtel describing her work in Hungary.

93 Ibid.

94 Flinck, A., Sambou S., & Uotila, E. (2012, June). Challenges and advantages of mediation in intimate relationship violence in Finland. Victim-offender mediation, an opportunity for change?

Mok, L.W.Y. (2012, June). The power of outreaching service for domestic violence abusers. A path to restorative justice in Chinese communities.

Both presentations at European Forum for Restorative Justice Conference, Connecting People: Victim, Offenders and Communities in Restorative Justice, Helsinki, Finland.

95 Porter, A. J. (2007). Restorative programs help hawaii inmates reconnect with community. *Restorative Practices eForum.* Bethlehem, PA: International Institute for Restorative Practices. Retrieved from http://www.iirp.edu/article_detail. php?article_id=NTU5

96 Burstein, C. & Heriza, T. (Producer/directors). (2009). *Concrete, steel and paint.* [55-minute DVD]. New Day Films: Harriman, N.Y. Available from http://www.concretefilm.org

97 Chapman, T. (2012, June). *Talking with political prisoners about their victims and desistance.* Presentation at European Forum for Restorative Justice Conference, Connecting People: Victim, Offenders and Communities in Restorative Justice, Helsinki, Finland.

98 Van Ness, D. (2005). Restorative justice in prisons. *Restorative Justice Online*. Washington D.C.: Centre for Justice and Reconciliation, Prison Fellowship International. Retrieved from http://www.restorativejustice.org/editions/2005/july05/2005-06-21.9036003387/view

99 Mirsky, L. (2010). Dreams from the monster factory: A restorative prison program for violent offenders. *Restorative Practices eForum*. Bethlehem, PA: International Institute for Restorative Practices. The article highlights the book by Schwartz S. (2009). *Dreams from the Monster Factory*. New York: Scribner. Retrieved from http://www.iirp.edu/article_detail.php?article_id=Njc1

100 McWhinnie, A. & Wilson, R. (2005). Courageous communities: Circles of support and accountability with individuals who have committed sexual offenses. *Restorative Practices eForum*. Bethlehem, PA: International Institute for Restorative Practices. Retrieved from http://www.iirp.edu/article_detail.php?article_id=NTIz

Miodownik, D. (2012, August). *That's my story and I'm sticking to it ... or am I?: Narratives, desistance and circles of support and accountability*. Presentation at Building a Restorative Practices Learning Network, IIRP 15th World Conference, Bethlehem, PA.

101 Van Lieshout, H. and Van Pagée, R. (2012, June) *Conferences in neighborhood conflicts*. Presentation at European Forum for Restorative Justice Conference, Connecting People: Victim, Offenders and Communities in Restorative Justice, Helsinki, Finland.

102 Vanfraechem, I. (2012, June). *Presentation of the Alternative-project*. European Forum for Restorative Justice Conference, Connecting People: Victim, Offenders and Communities in Restorative Justice, Helsinki, Finland.

103 Wachtel, J. (2009). Toward peace and justice in Brazil: Dominic Barter and restorative circles. *Restorative Practices eForum*. Bethlehem, PA: International Institute for Restorative

Practices. Retrieved from http://www.iirp.edu/article_detail. php?article_id=NjA2

Schmitz, Jean. (2012, August). *Restorative practices in neighborhoods in Lima, Peru.* Presentation at the 15th IIRP World Conference, Building a Restorative Practices Learning Network, Bethlehem, PA.

[104] Wachtel, J. (2013). Restorative justice for industrial pollution. *Restorative Practices eForum.* Bethlehem, PA: International Institute for Restorative Practices. Link for Youtube video from British Columbia, Canada, Ministry of Environment and Conservation Officer Service located on eForum web page. Retrieved from http://www.iirp.edu/article_detail. php?article_id=NDE2

[105] McCold, P. (2002); McCold, P. (2005); McCold, P. & Chang. A. (2008). Op. cit.

[106] Wachtel, T. (1999, February). *Restorative justice in everyday life: Beyond the formal process.* Paper presented at the Reshaping Australian Institutions Conference: Restorative Justice and Civil Society, The Australian National University, Canberra. Retrieved from http://www.iirp.edu/article_detail.php?article_id=NTAz

[107] Lewis, S. (2009). Op. cit.

[108] Macdonald, J. (2012). *Restorative Practices eForum.* Bethlehem, PA: International Institute for Restorative Practices. Retrieved from http://blog.iirp.edu/2012/01/restorative-city-hull-uk-takes-restorative-practices-to-the-private-sector/

[109] SaferSanerSchools: Whole-School Change Through Restorative Practices. (2011). Bethlehem, PA: International Institute for Restorative Practices. Retrieved from http://www.iirp.edu/pdf/WSC-Overview.pdf

[110] Gregory, A., Gerewitz, J., Clawson, K., David, A. & Korth, J. (2013, February). *RP-Observe Manual.* Uncirculated draft document. Rutgers University.

[111] Anderson, E. (1999). *Code of the Street: Decency Violence and the Moral Life of the Inner City.* New York: W.W. Norton & Company.

[112] Yardley, J. (1999, August 1). Book review of *Code of the Street: Decency Violence and the Moral Life of the Inner City* by Elijah Anderson. *The Washington Post.* Retrieved from http://www.amazon.com/Code-Street-Decency-Violence-Moral/dp/0393320782

[113] Mirsky, L. (2013). Using their words instead of their fists. *Restorative Practices eForum.* Bethlehem, PA: International Institute for Restorative Practices. Retrieved from http://blog.iirp.edu/2013/02/using-their-words-instead-of-their-fists/

[114] Strain, A.L. (2012, July 3). Restorative practices at home: A method used in some schools seems a useful tool in mommy's toolbox. San Carlos, CA: *San Carlos Patch.* Retrieved from: http://sancarlos.patch.com/articles/restorative-practices-at-home; also http://blog.iirp.edu/2012/07/on-restorative-parenting/

[115] Schott, M. In video clip. Retrieved from http://www.youtube.com/watch?v=PGcqDTqxif4

[116] Walker, M. In video. *The Transformation of West Philadelphia High School: A Story of Hope* (2009). Op. Cit.

[117] Edgar, K. & Newell T. (2006). *Restorative Justice in Prisons: A Guide to Making it Happen.* Winchester, UK: Waterside Press.

Swanson, C. (2009). *Restorative Justice in a Prison Community: Or Everything I Didn't Learn in Kindergarten I Learned in Prison.* Plymouth, UK: Lexington Books.

Van Ness, D. (2005). Op. cit.

[118] Maeppa, T. (2005). The Truth and Reconciliation Commission as a model of restorative justice. In Maeppa, T. (Ed.), *Beyond Retribution: Prospects for Restorative Justice in South Africa.* Retrieved from http://www.iss.co.za/pubs/Monographs/No111/Chap6.htm

[119] Gourevitch, P. (2009, May 4). The life after: Fifteen years after the genocide in Rwanda, the reconciliation defies expectations. *The New Yorker.* 36-39.

[120] Wachtel, J. (2006) John Braithwaite: Peacebuilder, social scientist and restorative justice activist. *Restorative Practices eForum.* Bethlehem, PA: International Institute for Restorative Practices. Retrieved from http://www.iirp.edu/article_detail.php?article_id=NTM0

[121] Braithwaite, J. (1999, august). *Democracy, community and problem solving.* Paper presented at the Strong Partnerships for Restorative Practices Conference, Burlington, Vermont. Retrieved from http://www.iirp.edu/article_detail.php?article_id=NDgz

[122] Costello, B., Wachtel, J. & Wachtel, T. (2010). *Restorative Circles in Schools: Building Community and Enhancing Learning.* Bethlehem, PA: International Institute for Restorative Practices.

[123] Ibid.

[124] Ibid.

[125] Thompson, W. I. (1971). *At the Edge of History: Speculations on the Transformation of Culture.* New York: Harper and Row.

[126] Peachey, D. (1989). The Kitchener experiment. In Wright, M. & Galaway, B. (Eds.), *Mediation and Criminal Justice: Victims, Offenders and Community.* London: Sage.

[127] Mirsky, L. (2003). The Wet'suwet'en Unlocking Aboriginal Justice Program: Restorative practices in British Columbia, Canada. *Restorative Practices eForum.* Bethlehem, PA: International Institute for Restorative Practices. Retrieved from http://www.iirp.edu/article_detail.php?article_id=NDE2

Educational Resources

To learn more about DVDs, books and
other resources provided by the IIRP,
please go to **www.iirp.edu/store**.

DVDs

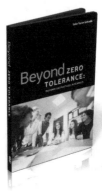

Beyond Zero Tolerance:
Restorative Practices in Schools

This 25-minute video documents the implementation of restorative practices in several schools in the USA, the Netherlands and Hull, England. The camera captures circles, conferences and one-on-one meetings in progress. Students, teachers and administrators speak candidly about the effects of restorative practices in their schools. The viewer is transported to bustling school hallways and classrooms and feels an unmistakable sense of lively and cheerful community. This vibrant and engrossing video is a powerful testament to the benefits of restorative practices in an educational setting.

Roundtable Discussions #1 & #2:
Restorative Strategies for Schools

Four expert practitioners of restorative practices discuss how to address a range of disciplinary and behavioral issues in schools. An ideal tool for administrators to raise their faculty's consciousness about restorative practices. Topics discussed include attendance issues, acting out in the classroom, bullying, working with parents, restorative consequences, favorite stories and dealing with difficult situations.

The Worst School I've Ever Been To

This video follows the stories of three students — Tim, Walt and Jamie — for an entire school year at a Community Service Foundation and Buxmont Academy alternative school/day treatment program for troubled youth in eastern Pennsylvania. A moving story about young people working to change their behavior and achieve their goals, the video is also instructive, showing a variety of restorative practices as they happen.

DVDs

Building Our Community:
A Film about Restorative Practices

Building Our Community is a documentary about the positive impact of restorative practices at Collingwood Primary School, in Hull, UK, a city facing some of the most acute economic and social challenges in England. Once a school in crisis, through the adoption of restorative practices Collingwood built a highly positive school culture and an exceptional sense of community, and helped pupils develop skills to feel respected, happy and able to make the most of their lives. This upbeat, informative video features interviews with teachers, students and parents sharing how they've benefited from the self-knowledge and empowerment developed during the restorative journey. The video is an engaging introduction to restorative practices in a school determined to give everyone a voice and a strong foundation for academic and emotional growth.

Four School Conferences: A Composite View

Four actual restorative conferences were videotaped at alternative schools operated by the Community Service Foundation and Buxmont Academy, sister nonprofit organizations serving troubled youth in eastern Pennsylvania. Footage from the conferences, held for offenses ranging from truancy and leaving school grounds to drug possession and bringing a knife onto a school bus, provide viewers with a realistic view of conferencing. Some conferences are highly emotional; others are not. Some conferences produce satisfying outcomes; others are less successful. But follow-up interviews with participants show that even a so-called "unsuccessful" conference can produce meaningful outcomes.

Visit **www.iirp.edu/store**

DVDs

Family Voices

"Family Voices" is an 18-minute documentary about family group decision making (FGDM), a restorative approach to problem solving used worldwide that enables families to make decisions for themselves, in child welfare, youth justice and other situations. In the empowering spirit of FGDM, "Family Voices" lets families do the talking. This moving, candid, even humorous video follows nine diverse American families on their journey of discovery of FGDM, from their initial fears, questions and hopes to their joy in seeing the process work. Children to grandparents offer their opinions and explain the FGDM process. It's an ideal vehicle to acquaint both families and professionals with FGDM.

Burning Bridges

"Burning Bridges" is a 35-minute documentary about the arson of Mood's Bridge, a historic covered bridge in Bucks County, Pennsylvania, USA, and the restorative conference held in its wake. The International Institute for Restorative Practices facilitated this emotional conference, which brought together the six young men who burned down the bridge with their families and members of the community. Using news footage, interviews and video of the actual conference, the documentary tells the story of a community moving through grief and anger to healing.

Toxic Talk

"Toxic Talk" shows an actual restorative conference following a workplace incident, in which staff members demeaned their supervisor behind her back and in the presence of customers. The conference, by providing everyone involved with a structured setting to express their emotions freely and honestly, transformed the negative feelings created by the incident into positive ones. The process restored relationships and created a healthier work environment.

DVDs

Facing the Demons

"Facing the Demons" documents the journey of the family and friends of murdered victim Michael Marslew, confronting face-to-face in a conference two of the offenders responsible for Michael's death.

Produced by the Dee Cameron Company, "Facing the Demons" won an award for "best television documentary of 1999" at the 2000 Logies Awards, the Australian equivalent of the Emmy Award, and in 2000 earned the United Nations Association Award for Best Television in its annual Media Peace Awards.

The 30-minute companion DVD "Commentary on Facing the Demons: The Facilitator's Perspective" — which includes commentary by Terry O'Connell, the Australian police sergeant who facilitated the dramatic conference — answers questions and addresses issues raised by the documentary.

A free 8-page study guide is available at:
www.iirp.edu/pdf/FacingTheDemonsStudyGuide.pdf

Conferencing for Serious Offenses: An Exploration

This thought-provoking, interactive, "do-it-yourself" seminar package provides DVDs (and a CD-ROM with printable Facilitator Guide and Participant Handout) for a group of professionals, students or others to examine the use of restorative conferencing in response to serious offenses.

The seminar package provides detailed directions for using the videos. Also included are instructions on how to run a "circle," which is the format used to structure discussion in the seminar. The use of the circle process provides a truly restorative experience that encourages active participation from everyone attending the seminar.

Please note: *This seminar is not intended to train participants to facilitate restorative conferences, but to enhance their understanding of the potential and the implications of conferencing for serious offenses.*

Visit **www.iirp.edu/store**

Books

The Restorative Practices Handbook
for Teachers, Disciplinarians and Administrators

This handbook is a practical guide for educators interested in implementing restorative practices, an approach that proactively builds positive school communities while dramatically reducing discipline referrals, suspensions and expulsions. The handbook discusses the spectrum of restorative techniques, offers implementation guidelines, explains how and why the processes work, and relates real-world stories of restorative practices in action.

Restorative Circles in Schools:
Building Community and Enhancing Learning

This book discusses the use of circles in schools and other settings and provides an in-depth exploration of circle processes. It includes numerous stories about the way circles have been used in many diverse situations, discussion on the use of proactive, responsive and staff circles, and an overview of restorative practices, with particular emphasis on its relationship to circle processes.

Restorative Justice Conferencing:
Real Justice® and The Conferencing Handbook

Two books in one volume, "Restorative Justice Conferencing" includes (1) the official training manual that provides a step-by-step guide to setting up and conducting restorative justice conferences and (2) actual conference stories to show how conferencing works and how it can change the way our society responds to wrongdoing in schools, criminal justice, the workplace and elsewhere.

Books

Family Power:
Engaging and Collaborating with Families

"Family Power" offers practical guidance for engaging and collaborating with families, illustrated by anecdotes gathered from professionals in a range of settings around the world. The authors connect FGC/FGDM with the broader field of restorative practices, which holds that "people are happier, more cooperative and productive, and more likely to make positive changes when those in positions of authority do things *with* them, rather than *to* them or *for* them."

Building Campus Community:
Restorative Practices in Residential Life

"Building Campus Community" offers effective strategies and a guiding philosophy that enable college and universities to foster positive relationships, respond to conflicts and problems and raise consciousness about bias, alcohol abuse and other critical campus issues. It includes comprehensive implementation guidelines as well as numerous true stories — some enlightening, some comical, some poignant — about how the practices are being applied in higher education.

Safer Saner Schools:
Restorative Practices in Education

This collection of articles from the Restorative Practices eForum — the IIRP's internet publication with thousands of subscribers around the world — conveys the power of restorative practices to transform schools into positive, vibrant communities while dramatically reducing discipline referrals, detentions and suspensions. The articles include accounts of personal experiences, implementation and research in schools from the United States and Canada to the United Kingdom, Europe, Australia and Asia.

Visit **www.iirp.edu/store**

Other Resources

Restorative Questions Poster

This 18" x 24" poster, designed for use in classrooms, prominently displays the essential restorative questions for easy reference in the event of a conflict or harmful incident. The top has questions used to respond to challenging behavior; the bottom has questions to help those harmed by others' actions.

Restorative Questions Sign

This rugged, portable 20" x 35" A-frame sign is designed for use in schools and on playgrounds. It prominently displays the essential restorative questions for easy reference in the event of a conflict or harmful incident. One side has questions used to respond to challenging behavior; the other has questions to help those harmed by others' actions.

Restorative Questions Cards

This pack of 100 handy two-sided coated 2" x 3.5" cards puts the essential restorative questions at your fingertips. One side has questions used to respond to challenging behavior; the other has questions to help those harmed by others' actions. The cards fit easily in a wallet.

IIRP Globe Ball

This small, squeezable globe ball is perfect for use as a talking piece in restorative circles.

Restorative Works
learning network

Restorative Works — a project of the Restorative Practices Foundation, in collaboration with the International Institute for Restorative Practices Graduate School — offers free educational content, news and announcements to help people become more knowledgeable and proficient in restorative practices.

Sign up for the Restorative Practices eForum, the voice of Restorative Works, to receive email updates.

restorativeworks.net

About the IIRP

The International Institute for Restorative Practices (IIRP) is the world's first graduate school wholly dedicated to the emerging field of restorative practices. The IIRP is engaged in the advanced education of professionals at the graduate level and to the conduct of research that can develop the growing field of restorative practices, with the goal of positively influencing human behavior and strengthening civil society.

The Graduate School offers flexible master's degree and certificate options through a mix of hybrid and online graduate courses, independent study and professional development events held around the world. Students may complete a graduate program with little or no travel required to the IIRP campus in Bethlehem, Pennsylvania.

As the world's leading provider of restorative practices education, the IIRP has delivered professional development for tens of thousands of individuals from more than 55 countries working in education, criminal justice, and social and human services. To learn more about the IIRP Graduate School, go to **www.iirp.edu**.

About the Author

Ted Wachtel is the president and founder of the International Institute for Restorative Practices (iirp.edu), an accredited master's degree-granting graduate school. Wachtel and his wife, Susan, also founded the Community Service Foundation and Buxmont Academy (csfbuxmont.org), which operate schools, counseling and residential programs in Pennsylvania, employing restorative practices with delinquent and at-risk youth. Wachtel has written and produced numerous books and films on restorative practices and other topics. He has done keynote presentations and workshops on restorative justice and restorative practices at conferences and events around the world.